Stock-Market Arithmetic

Stock-Market Arithmetic: A Primer for New Investors

Charles J. Caes

Regnery Books
Chicago

Contents

To my wife, Karen, for all her support,
in this and every project

Preface

This book simplifies the arithmetic used in the business of buying and selling securities.

Brevity and clarity should be the rules for every learning exercise, and they are for this book, which has been prepared for students of all ages from the sophomore in high school to the senior citizen considering the stock market for the first time.

The book proceeds on the assumption that the reader has virtually no knowledge of what the stock market is about other than the fact that it represents an opportunity for investors to make or lose money.

If you purchased this book because you are seeking a fundamental understanding of the arithmetic of stock purchases, you have made a worthwhile investment.

Additionally, you should note that there are many investment vehicles and related techniques which are available to small and large investors alike. "Playing the market" means not only the purchase and sale of corporate stock, but dealing in and with these vehicles (such as options, convertibles, warrants, etc.), as well. This book, however, has been prepared for the beginning student, and, as the saying goes, first things first. Thus, except for a general description of options and warrants in Chapter 9 and general reference to other investment strategies, these other forms of investing in the market have been left for future studies.

1

The Stock Market

When people talk about the stock market what they are actually referring to is that market for corporate stocks which is created by the various stock exchanges around the world. Stock exchanges are actually auction markets which provide a convenient means through which individuals can invest in business enterprises at almost any time. (Table 1.1 shows stock sales on registered exchanges, 1960–79).

In the United States informal exchanges have existed since the early part of the 18th century, having been begun and cultivated right in New York City. But in those earlier days the exchanges dealt not only in corporate stocks and certain commodities but also in human beings; slave traders were as much a part of those early exchanges as were the usual merchants and brokers. The first truly organized exchange in the United States was actually established in Philadelphia in the year 1790. The members of this exchange proved to be a well-managed group and this exchange was, for many years, far ahead of that loosely knit group of New York auctioneers who never really organized their operation formally and thus for decades were not able to surpass their Philadelphia counterparts. It was as early as 1792, however, when that New York group of brokers began to charge fees for representing others in the purchase and sale of corporate stocks.

Back in those days, New York was hardly the metropolis that it is today; its population had not yet reached 50,000. Once this fact is realized, it is no surprise to learn that the first indoor headquarters for these merchants and traders was a coffee house—the Tontine Coffee House.

As this nation of ours began to grow, government obligations increased markedly and so, too, did the banking and insurance communities. And in the 25 years since that informal start in 1790 there was created such interest in stocks and bonds that the brokerage community also grew steadily and wealthy. Before long it was clear to securities dealers that

Table 1.1
Sales of Stocks on Registered Exchanges
1960–79

Year	Market Value ($ billion)	Shares (millions)
1960	45	1,389
1965	89	2,587
1970	131	4,539
1973	179	5,723
1974	118	4,846
1975	157	6,231
1976	195	7,036
1977	187	7,023
1978	249	9,483
1979	300	10,863

From a table in the 1980 *Statistical Abstract of the United States*, p. 545. Original source: U.S. Securities & Exchange Commission.

what was needed was a constitution to both guide their business activities and limit their membership. They drafted that constitution, put that limit on membership, and called themselves the "New York Stock Exchange Board." From that time on each new member would have to be sponsored by a present member and his application would have to be approved by the entire membership.

As conditions continued to become more and more crowded, the members of the New York Stock Exchange Board decided that it would be necessary to rent indoor quarters and they subsequently made 40 Wall St. their first real home. By this time they were charging new members a membership fee; that fee was based on exactly where the newcomer's seat would be located in the trading room. They also levied fines and expelled those who did not adhere to the rules.

Today, on any of the exchanges, there are no seats. In fact, the exchanges today bear hardly any resemblance to old 40 Wall St. But the term "seat" is still used.

With the advent of the Civil War, new interest was created in the securities market. Creation or improvement of any market attracts greater numbers of entrepreneurs. Accordingly, applications for "seats" in the exchange skyrocketed. Not all applicants could be accepted, however. Memberships had to be limited.

Not to be lost to any money-making opportunity, those brokers on whom the door was shut organized their own exchange which they called the "Open Board of Brokers." There was competition for awhile, but the two exchanges were soon to merge into what today is known as the "New York Stock Exchange."

At the time this exchange was created, there was another group of brokers who had been conducting business in the open since 1849. They were the hard-dealing members of the New York Curb Exchange. "Curb" was a fitting part of the name, since that exchange's members were literally conducting business—actually buying and selling securities—right on the sidewalk curb. This little group of businessmen continued to do their business with the sky for a roof until they finally moved their exchange indoors in 1921. Now the New York Curb Exchange is the American Stock Exchange.

Today the New York Stock Exchange and the American Stock Exchange are only two of many exchanges here in the United States. These exchanges, it might be noted, do not actually buy and sell securities and they do not set the price at which the securities will sell. All trading takes place among the membership; the exchanges simply provide the administrative and clerical assistance needed for trading activities.

All trading at any of these exchanges can only be conducted by the exchange's members, and membership is always strictly limited. Membership still can only be obtained by purchasing another member's seat on an exchange.

An applicant has a choice of a number of types of memberships on an exchange. There are memberships for commission brokers, floor brokers, registered traders, specialists, odd-lot dealers, and block positioners.

Commission brokers handle buy-and-sell transactions for the general public. Their fee is a percentage of the amount of the transaction.

Floor brokers conduct transactions for other members

of the same exchange in return for a commission. These floor brokers serve an important roll as backups for the other brokers. They handle excess orders that otherwise could not be handled at all or efficiently and they fill in for other brokers when those brokers cannot be available.

Registered traders are members of an exchange who buy and sell securities for their own account. They neither handle orders for other brokers nor do they handle orders for the general public. They buy a seat and pay the related costs so they can personally buy and sell for their own profit. Strict parameters are established to guide these registered traders so that their activities will in no way conflict with the trading public.

Specialists handle "limit" orders for other brokers. This is to say that if a customer has given instructions to his broker to buy a stock currently selling at $11.50 for no more than $10.00, the broker will call on a specialist to "stay with" the stock and execute the order at the very first opportunity which is presented. Specialists have another and very important responsibility. This is to maintain what is called an "orderly market." To do this they must buy and sell for their own accounts whenever there is an unusual trading situation developing.

Odd-lot dealers are those exchange members who buy from or sell to customers of commission brokers dealing in fewer than 100 shares. These odd-lot dealers do not work on a usual-type commission. Rather, they earn their income on the difference between buy and sell prices on the shares they may be trading.

Block positioners handle trades of $200,000 or more in a particular stock.

Review Questions

The statements below are either true or false; indicate which.

1. The stock market is that market for corporate stocks created by national and local exchanges around the world.

2. Since the 1700s, small, informal exchanges have existed in the United States.

3. In their early days, stock exchanges not only dealt in corporate stocks but also in the slave trade.

4. The first organized exchange in the United States was established in Philadelphia in the year 1790.

5. The New York Stock Exchange was originally called the New York Curb Exchange.

6. There is now only one exchange in the United States: The New York Stock Exchange.

7. Floor brokers conduct transactions for other members of the same exchange in return for a commission.

8. Registered brokers are members of an exchange who buy and sell securities for their account.

9. Odd-lot dealers are those exchange members who buy from, or sell to, customers of commission brokers dealing in fewer than 100 shares.

10. Block positioners handle trades of $200,000 or more in a particular stock.

Answers to Review Questions will be found beginning on page 97.

2

Stock Quotations

More often than not, if you decide to buy or sell stock in a corporation you will do your business through a stockbroker who, in turn, will make the purchases for you through one of the many organizations which make a market for corporate stocks. These organizations are exchanges like those discussed in Chapter 1. There are many exchanges here in the United States and also many exchanges in other countries.

The largest exchange in the United States is the New York Stock Exchange. The second largest is the American Stock Exchange. Other widely known, though much smaller exchanges stateside are the Midwest, Boston, Pacific, and Philadelphia. Sometimes you will find that more than one exchange is listing a particular corporation's stock.

Each exchange has its own requirements for the stock which it is willing to list, and these requirements will vary widely. Just knowing what exchange a stock is listed on gives some seasoned investors an idea of its investment characteristics.

For instance, if an investor notes that a company's stock is listed on the New York Stock Exchange, he knows that:

1. the company has attracted a great deal of national interest;
2. the company has a relatively strong position, as well as stability, in its industry;
3. the company's market is an expanding one and it has the ability to expand right along with it.

He also knows that in all probability, the company has:
1. the capability of earning, in a competitive market, and before deductions for federal income taxes, at least $2.5 million; it also has recorded earnings in each of the past two years of at least $2 million before taxes;
2. at least $16 million in net tangible assets;

3. at least a million common shares held by the public;
4. at least 2,000 stockholders owning 100 shares or more of its stock.

Fig. 2.1
Stock Market Quotations

52-Week High	52-Week Low	Stock	Div A	Yld % B	PE Ratio C	Sales 100s D	High	Low	Last	Chg.
39½	29⅛	ACF	2.24	6.4	7	339	35¼	34⅞	34⅞	. .
23⅜	15⅜	AMF	1.24	7.3	7	617	17¼	16⅞	16⅞–	⅜
32⅞	13	AM Intl	.28	1.8	6	188	15⅜	14¾	15¼–	. .
14¾	8⅞	APL	1.00	9.3	. . .	29	10⅞	10	10¾	. .
48⅜	33¾	ARA	1.64	4.6	7	591	35½	34⅝	35⅜+	¾
31⅜	20½	ASA	1.40	5.3	. . .	285	26⅞	26½	26½–	¼
14⅞	8½	ATO	.48	4.5	4	197	11⅛	10⅝	10⅝–	⅜
34⅞	17	AVX	.50	1.5	11	48	32⅝	32	32½–	¼
40	29½	AbbtLb	1.00	3.0	13	584	33½	33	33⅜	. .
23¾	16¼	AcmeC	1.20	5.8	6	60	21	20½	20¾+	¼
6¼	3⅜	AdmDg	.04	1.0	6	25	4	4	4	. .
13	10¾	AdaEx	1.28e	3.9	7	7	11¾	11½	11⅝–	⅛
8½	3⅞	AdmMI	.20e	3.9	7	7	5⅛	5⅛	5⅛	. .
33¼	28⅝	AetnaLf $	1.80	5.6	5	887	33⅛	32¼	32¼–	⅝
28¼	17⅝	Ahmans	1.20	4.4	5	152	28¼	27½	27½–	⅝
4	2	Alleen		. . .	. . .	5	2¾	2⅝	2⅝	. .

Figure 2.1 gives a partial listing of stock market quotations. Let's take a close look at these quotes in order to interpret some of the transactions which the listing shows have taken place.

But first note that the fractional parts of the quotations which are listed are in eights, fourths, and halves of a dollar. We are, actually, counting by 12-½,

⅛ = 12-½ cents
²⁄₈ (¼) = 25 cents
⅜ = 37-½ cents

$$\frac{4}{8} \, (\frac{1}{2}) = 50 \text{ cents}$$
$$\frac{5}{8} = 62\text{-}\frac{1}{2} \text{ cents}$$
$$\frac{6}{8} \, (\frac{3}{4}) = 75 \text{ cents}$$
$$\frac{7}{8} = 87\text{-}\frac{1}{2} \text{ cents}$$

Bearing this in mind, let's zero in on Figure 2.1 and check the action in ACF Industries. Column by column now:

52-Week High. This price ($39.50) represents the highest price at which the stock was sold during the past 52 weeks. That high, however, does not represent the present day's listing, so if ACF reaches a new high today, it would not change the number in this column, not until the next day's listing.

52-Week Low. This price ($29.12-½) represents the lowest price at which the stock was sold during the past 52 weeks. This low, however, does not represent the present day's listing, so if ACF reaches a new low today, it would not change the number in this column, not until the next day's listing.

Stock. In this column appears the name of the stock, which is usually abbreviated.

Div (dividend). This amount ($2.24) indicates the total amount of dividends the company is expected to declare on each share of stock. If you own one share of stock, you can expect to receive from the company $2.24 over the coming year, although you will receive it in quarterly payments of $.56 each.

Yld (yield) %. This is the annual rate of return, expressed as a percentage, which the purchaser would receive if he pruchased the stock at the present price. For example, ACF is paying out in dividends $2.24 per year. The current price of the stock is $34.87-½. (This may also be expressed as $34.875.) The yield is determined by dividing the dividend ($2.24) by the current price ($34.875). The result of this division is .0642294.

Rounding the result to the third position (.064), we then express it in percent: 6.4.

PE Ratio. This is the price-earning ratio. It is determined by dividing the current market price of a share of stock by the earnings per share. Since the earnings per share are not listed in stock quotations, the PE ratio listed in the quotations will help you determine what the earnings are. Simply divide the closing price of the stock by the PE ratio; the result is the approximate earnings per share—"approximate" because the PE ratio is given rounded to the nearest whole number.

Sales 100s. The number in this column represents how many hundreds of shares were traded for ACF on the day for which quotations are given. Thus, the 339 in this column actually represents 33,900 (339 × 100) shares.

High, Low, Last. The dollar values in these columns represent the highest and lowest prices at which ACF traded for the day and the last price at which ACF traded.

Chg. (Change). The number in this column represents the difference—plus, minus, or no change at all—between the last price quoted for the present day's listing and the last price quoted for the previous day's listing. For ACF there was no change. The stock closed on this day at exactly the same price it closed the day before.

What do we know about ACF stock? We know for the last 52 weeks it has been selling between $29-⅛ and $39-½ per share. We also know that if we had purchased it as its closing price for the day ($34-⅞) the dividend alone would bring us a 6.4 percent return on our money. We also know that it is a fairly active issue, having traded some 33,900 shares. But is the stock priced too high? Or is it at bargain prices? A lot more research is required before these questions can be answered. You would have to take a look at the stock's history, the present economic environment in general, the economic environment for those industries of which ACF is a part, and try to gather from your broker or some other analyst just what the projected earnings may be.

But even with all this information, you couldn't be guaranteed that your decision will be the correct one. You would also want to check investor interest in the stock, whether it's a take-over candidate, whether its management is strong or weak, what its financing needs may be in the future, what its book value is, what its balance sheet has to say. As you will realize from some of the sample transactions which are presented in Chapter 5, you do not buy or sell stocks when your entire research has been nothing more than a glance at the present day's listing. It is not that simple.

Stock quotations that we find in the financial sections of newspapers actually tell us a bit more than has been explained so far through the use of alphabetical symbols or abbreviations.

In the price columns there may be additional alphamerics (letters, numbers, other symbols and marks) indicating that a price represents a high or a low trading price for the year. In the dividend column there may be footnotes representing extra payouts besides the regular dividend; additional stock dividends; liquidating dividends (dividends paid as a result of selling the assets of a company); dividends paid in some foreign currency.

Let's take a look now at some transactions, just to get used to using the tables and working with fractions. We'll concentrate here on determining the cost to purchase stock (before commissions, which will be discussed later) and computing dividends.

Example No. 1. You buy 200 shares of ACF at the high of the day; (a) how much did the shares cost you and (b) what is the total amount of dividends you will receive based on the current payment?

a) 200 shares × $35-¼ =
200 shares × $35.25 =
$7,050 total cost.

b) 200 shares × $2.24 =
$448.00 per year in dividends.

Regardless, then, of whether or not the value of the stock goes up or down, as long as there is no change in the dividend payout, you will receive $448.00 per year from this investment.

Example No. 2. You buy 25 shares of AMF Corporation (see Fig. 2.1) at the low of the day; (a) how much did the shares cost you, and (b) what is the total amount of dividends you will receive based on the current payment?

a) 25 shares × $16-⅞ =
25 shares × $16.87-½ =
25 shares × $16.875 =
$421.875 =
$421.88.

b) 25 shares × $1.24 =
$31.00 per year in dividends.

Once again, whether or not the value of the stock goes up or down, as long as there is no change in the dividend payout, you will receive $31.00 per year from this investment.

Review Questions

Questions 1–3 are either true or false; indicate which.

1. The largest exchange in the United States is the New York Stock Exchange.

2. Yield is the annual (unless otherwise specified) rate of return.

3. PE ratio refers to the number of times by which the company's latest 12-month earnings must be multiplied to obtain the current stock price.

4. Convert the following fractions to parts of a dollar:

a. ⅛
b. ¼
c. ⅜
d. ⅝
e. 1-¼

5. You buy 200 shares of XYZ Corp. at $20-½. The company pays an annual dividend of $.50 per share. How much in dividends will you receive each year from XYZ?

3

Brokerage Fees

When you buy or sell stock through a stockbroker you must pay a commission (brokerage fee) each time you buy and each time you sell stock. The exact amount of the fee depends upon the number of shares that are bought and sold and whether the shares are traded in odd or round lots. A round lot refers to multiples of 100 shares, and an odd lot is anything less than 100 shares.

Brokerage fees will vary considerably. In recent years there has been a proliferation of discount houses which offer bare-bones services and which charge their customers very low trading commissions. On the other end of the spectrum are the larger and more service-oriented brokerage houses which not only handle a customer's buy and sell orders but also publish and distribute a wealth of material to help in selecting stocks with strong potential.

In the examples of buy-and-sell transactions which are presented in the next chapter, the commission rates are arbitrarily selected, for we are not as concerned with the procedures for computing brokerage fees as we are in how those brokerage fees subtract from profits and add to losses in stock trades.

Brokerage firms charge a minimum fee for executing orders, and those minimums will vary little from brokerage house to brokerage house. Thus, on small odd-lot orders you will find yourself paying a rather high percentage in commissions. For example, if you were to sell 15 shares of stock at $25-1/8, the commission, based on one broker's schedule, would be about $30.00. That is almost 8 percent in commissions. Under the same price structure you could sell 100 shares of stock at $11.00 and pay only about $35.00. In this last case the commission amounts to only about 3 percent.

Brokerage fees are always being revised, so it is very hard to talk in specifics. By the time this book gets into your hands there's no telling what the fees for executing your orders will be. The table on which we are basing brokerage fees for our examples may or may not be near the current averages. The important thing to remember is that these fees must be considered in determining where your break-even point will be in buy-and-sell transactions.

In the transactions and exercises which appear in this and following chapters, the brokerage commissions will be supplied. And for purposes of simplification, brokerage fees and other related costs will all be grouped together and referred to as "fees."

Having that fee schedule at hand before buying and selling is always a good idea. Without it you may decide to sell a stock at a price at which you believe you will achieve at least a marginal profit. But after all fees are deducted from or added to a transaction, you may very well find yourself with a loss rather than a gain.

If you buy 100 shares of stock at $12.00 per share, and one year later sell it at $12.50 per share, at first calculation it appears that you have made a $50.00 profit. But if the fees on both the buy and sell orders amounted to $78.00—zappo, you've a loss of $28.00 after tieing up your money for a year.

If you buy and sell securities fairly regularly, your annual costs for brokerage fees can well add up to thousands of dollars, and that of course reduces your profits considerably.

Savings in brokerage commissions can add to your profits; and brokerage information and research services can help you select the right stocks. So it pays to shop around for a broker who offers you exactly the right combination of price and services to help you win in the market.

Review Questions

1. If you buy 100 shares of stock for $10.00 per share and sell it six months later for $10-¼ per share, what is your profit before commissions?

2. If you buy 100 shares of stock for $10.00 per share and sell it five months later for $10-½ per share, how much is your profit (or loss) if your buy and sell commissions total $65.00?

3. About where would your break-even point be if you purchased 200 shares of stock at $9.00 per share and the buy commissions were $53.00? (Remember to approximate fees for the sell transaction.)

4. Will savings in brokerage commissions really enhance your profits if you trade frequently?

5. Must you pay a brokerage commission even if you take a loss on a stock transation?

4

Rate of Return

Investors will purchase stock for a number of reasons. But, of course, in the final analysis they've but one goal in mind, and that goal is to make as much money as they can. Many purchase stock for the purpose of selling it later at a higher price. Others purchase stock because they find the dividends being paid offer them a higher rate of return on their investment than they would receive in a bank savings account. Others will invest both for the profit they may receive on buy-and-sell transactions as well as for the rate of return they will receive on their money (via dividends) while they wait for the price of that stock to climb.

The money a bank distributes to its savings depositors is called "interest." However, the share of profits that a bank, or any corporation, may distribute to its shareholders is called "dividends." But all stocks do not pay dividends and even if they have been paying dividends, there is no guarantee that they will continue to do so. The determining factors in whether or not a dividend will be paid are the issuing corporation's continued success and/or whether or not the board of directors decides to share profits with stockholders or just reinvest the money back into their corporation.

The dividend paid to the stockholder represents a return on his investment, and as such it is often expressed as a percent value, and referred to as the "rate of return." Another term for rate of return is "yield." The yield is determined by dividing the amount invested in a company's stock into the annual dividends. You've already read how this is done in Chapter 2 under "Yield %" but for further clarification, here are some additional examples.

Example No. 1. You invest $1,000 in a stock that pays an annual dividend of $100.00 per year on your investment. What is your rate of return?

Rate of Return (Yield) = Dividend divided by Cost
= $100.00 ÷ $1,000*
= .10 (or 10%)

Example No. 2. You purchase 100 shares of ACF Industries at $35.25 per share. Annual dividends are $2.24. What will be your rate of return?

$2.24 ÷ $35.25 = .064 (or 6.4%)

In each of the previous examples, the brokerage and other related fees have not been considered in the calculation. They usually are not until after the stock is sold and the investor is interested in determining what was his total return for the period in which he held the stock. But some investors will include the buy commissions in their calculations for a more accurate picture of their rate of return, and then recalculate again after the sale of the stock.

Example No. 3. You have purchased 100 shares of ACF at $35.25 per share. You receive four (4) dividend payments totalling $324.00 and then sell the stock after 13 months for a $100.00 profit. Brokerage and related fees come to $130.00. What was your true rate of return?

(100 shares × $35.25) + $130.00 = $3,655.00 total cost
$324.00 (total div. + cap. gain**) ÷ $3,655.00 = .0886 (8.86%) rate of return

An interesting thing to note is that you do not have to own shares of stock for an entire quarter to receive dividends due for that period. Neither do you have to keep a stock for an entire year to be eligible for the annual payout. Very often you may own the stock for only a couple of weeks or even days and yet be eligible for the quarterly, semiannual, or

*This is the way the operation would be performed on a calculator.
**Bear in mind that profits from the sale of stock (capital gains) and dividends are treated differently for tax purposes.

annual payout. As long as you purchased the stock before the ex-dividend date you are eligible for the coming dividend payment.

By "ex-dividend" is meant "without dividend." This is to say that a stock selling ex-dividend is being sold without the rights to the coming dividend. For transfer and record purposes, every stock on which a dividend is declared will have an ex-dividend period. This is because provisions must be made to allow enough time for the delivery of the stock. Usually, the time allowed is four days.

For example, suppose a dividend is declared payable to holders of record listed on the company's books on, say, May 11. Since four days must be scheduled to allow for delivery of the stock, the stock would be declared ex-dividend beginning May 7. Anyone who purchases the stock after May 7 will not be entitled to the coming dividend.

Buyers of stocks usually make note of ex-dividend dates, for, generally, unless they are short-term speculators, they are interested in the yield—or total rate of return—they will receive from their investment.

The *rate of return*, by the way, should not be confused with what is termed the *dividend rate*. These terms mean entirely two different things, and to thoroughly distinguish them let's discuss the two kinds of stock a corporation will issue.

Actually, there are many kinds of stock that a corporation issues, but, generally speaking, they may be divided into two classifications: common stock and preferred stock. In most cases, the preferred stock holder gets *preference* when corporate profits are distributed. Therefore, when dividends are declared they are distributed to preferred stockholders and then (if there are any left to be distributed) to common stockholders. The annual rate of interest paid on the preferreds is based on the par value of the stock, whereas in the case of common stock the remainder of the profits is simply divided evenly by share. Preferred stocks generally pay higher dividends, as illustrated in Table 4.1.

Par value is an arbitrary value assigned to a share of stock by company directors. In the case of preferred issues, it becomes the multiplicand in the operation to establish the dollar return an investor can expect based on the preferred's rate. This is to say that if an investor owns 100 shares of an 8 percent preferred, *$100 par*, he may expect to receive up to $800.00 per year on his investment. We say "up to" because this return on investment can vary—depending upon decisions by the board of directors.

Table 4.1
Yields on Preferred
and Common Stocks
1970–79

Year	Preferred (10 stocks in % per year)	Common (in % per year)	
		Composite (500 stocks)	Industrials (400 stocks)
1970	7.22	3.83	3.62
1972	6.88	2.84	2.61
1973	7.23	3.06	2.79
1974	8.24	4.47	4.13
1975	8.36	4.31	3.96
1976	7.98	3.77	3.48
1977	7.61	4.62	4.43
1978	8.25	5.28	5.06
1979	9.11	5.47	5.20

From a table in the *1980 Statistical Abstract of the United States*, p. 545.

Common stocks need not be assigned a par value at authorization. When they are not, they are listed on the books at market value.

For both preferred and common stock, it is important to remember that the true value is what someone else is willing to pay for it—and, therefore, the true worth is whatever the quoted bid price is for a share of the stock.

If you purchase a 5% preferred stock which has a par value of $100.00, then your annual dividend on each share is $5.00. The 5% is your dividend rate (5% × $100.00 = $5.00).

The value of the preferred in the market place may go way above or way below $100.00, but the dividend will always be $5.00. The dividend rate on the par value will always remain 5%; the true yield based on the present value of the stock, however, will change according to the ratio of the market value of the stock to the amount of the dividend.

Your rate of return, then, is the annual dividend divided by what you actually paid for the stock in the market place. You see, although the preferred stock has a par value of $100.00, you may very well have purchased each share at an average of $95.00 per share. Therefore, while the dividend rate was 5% (of par value), your actual rate of return is $5.00 divided by $95.00, the result of which is .053 or 5.3%.

Example No. 4. You purchase 50 shares of a 6% preferred stock. Par value is $100.00. You paid a total of $5,150, including fees, to purchase the stock. What is your rate of return?

$$6\% \times \$100.00 \qquad = \$6.00 \text{ per share annual dividend}$$
$$\$6.00 \times 50 \text{ shares} = \$300.00 \text{ total annual dividend}$$
$$\$300.00 \div \$5,150 \quad = .0582 \text{ or } 5.82\%^{*}$$

Example No. 5. You purchase 100 shares of a 5% preferred stock. Par value is $25.00. You paid a total of $2,375, including fees, to purchase the stock. What is your rate of return?

$$5\% \times \$25.00 \qquad = \$1.25 \text{ per share dividend}$$
$$\$1.25 \times 100 \text{ shares} = \$125.00 \text{ total annual dividend}$$
$$\$125.00 \div \$2,375 \quad = .0526 \text{ or } 5.26\%$$

As you have noticed, the procedures for determining the rate of return on preferred stock are to find the amount of the dividend, then divide that amount by the price of the stock.

*You may also simply divide the dividend per share by the cost per share, but this will give you a slightly inflated rate of return, since it does not include fees.

Review Exercises

1. Determine the rate of return for each transaction below, each of which represents a common stock purchase.

Cost of Shares	Annual Dividends	Rate of Return
$950.00	$45.00	?
$2,500	$125.00	?
$6,000	$295.00	?

2. Determine the rate of return for each of the transactions below, each of which represents a preferred stock purchase of 100 shares.

Cost of Shares	Par Value	Dividend Rate	Rate of Return
$9,100	$100.00	4½%	?
$5,000	$50.00	5%	?
$6,200	$50.00	6%	?

Final day of trading on the old trading floor, April 26, 1901. This was the first permanent home of the New York Stock Exchange. The building was located at 10 Broad Street. Opened in 1865, it was designed by John Kellum and redesigned by James Renwick from 1869–71. (Courtesy N.Y. Stock Exchange Archives)

5

Making and Losing Money

Believe it or not, you can play the market to go up or you can play it to go down.

When you play the market to go up, or you're expecting an individual stock to move higher, you are being "bullish." A "bull" takes what is called a "long" position in a stock. That means he has purchased a company's stock and his investment plan is to hold onto it until it increases to a certain value.

When you play the market to go down, or you're expecting an individual stock to move lower, you are being "bearish." A "bear" takes what is called a "short" position in a stock. This means he sells the stock before he buys it. How does he do this? First, he tells his broker that he wants to "sell short" on a particular stock and he places his order.* The broker, in turn, borrows the shares to be sold and holds them until the investor decides to buy them back. Now everything works in reverse. Each ⅛ of a point that the stock goes up, the bear loses money. But each ⅛ of a point that the stock goes down, the bear makes money.

Now, let's look at some hypothetical situations and see how money is made and lost in the market place. The first series of transactions presented will be bullish; this is to say that the investors will actually buy the shares in anticipation of their increasing in value. The next series of transactions will be bearish; that is, the investors will be playing certain stocks to go down in value so they will make a profit.

Mr. John Phelps

The first investor you must meet is Mr. John Phelps, a very thrifty young man. But he's dissatisfied with the interest

---

*A margin account is required (see chap. 6) and a bear is required to deposit in his account at least 50 percent of the value of the stock he has sold.

his money has been earning in the local savings bank. He feels that if he were to invest his money *successfully* in the stock market, he could better keep up with inflation. The 6-½ percent he's getting on his savings just isn't enough. So he withdraws about $5,000 from his account and invests in the stock market.

Transaction No. 1. On September 15, 1981, John Phelps takes his first shot at the market and buys 300 shares of stock in an aviation firm, which we will call Company A. His costs:

300 shares at $13.50	= $4,050.00
Fees	97.00
Total Cost	$4,147.00

Note that his actual cost per share was $13.82 ($4,147 divided by 300 shares) after commissions. But Phelps thought this all peanuts compared to what he would earn when the shares doubled in price.

Transaction No. 2. A little more than one month later, the shares of this same aviation company take a bit of a tumble and are now worth only $11.00. Phelps decides to sell out, fearing that the shares will depreciate even further. He sells at $11.00.

300 shares at $11.00	= $3,300.00
Fees	90.00
Amount Received	$3,210.00

After fees were deducted, Phelps actually had received only $10.70 for each share.

SCOREBOARD

Bought 300 shares of Company A at	$4,147
Sold 300 shares of Company A at	3,210
Total Capital Loss	$ 937

Transaction No. 3. The newspapers announce that a financial company wants to take over a publishing company and the talk on the street is that the publishing company's stock could very well double in just days. Phelps decides to take a chance and purchase stock in the publishing company, which we will call Company B. He gets the shares at $31-¾ apiece.

100 shares at $31-¾	= $3,175.00
Fees	65.00
Total Cost	$3,240.00

Transaction No. 4. Negotiations between the two companies fell apart and the market place loses interest. The result is that the shares Phelps holds fall sharply. Phelps has held the stock long enough to collect 25 cents per share in dividends but then finally bails out when the stock is at $25-¼.

100 shares at $25-¼	= $2,525.00
Fees	60.00
Amount Received	$2,465.00

SCOREBOARD

Bought 300 shares of Company A at	$4,147	
Sold 300 shares of Company A at	3,210	
Capital Loss		($ 937.00)
Bought 100 shares of Company B at	$3,240	
Sold 100 shares of Company B at	2,465	
Capital Loss		($ 775.00)
Total Capital Losses		($1,712.00)
Less Dividend Income (Company B)		25.00
		($1,687.00)

Poor Mr. Phelps. He had been earning better than 6 percent on his money. Now he is losing hundreds. Well, if he is smart enough to pick a strong mover next time, he just might make up his losses or even turn a profit.

Transaction No. 5. Mr. Phelps now decides to buy 100 shares of stock in a retail store which, for convenience, we will refer to as Company C. He gets the shares for $17-⅝ per share.

100 shares at $17.625	= $1,762.50
Fees	44.00
Total Cost	$1,806.50

Transaction No. 6. After holding the shares for awhile, Mr. Phelps decided that his market timing was poor and Company C will not increase in share value for some time. He manages to sell the shares for exactly the same price at which he purchased them: $17-⅝.

100 shares at $17.625	= $1,762.50
Fees	46.34
Amount Received	$1,716.16

Despite the fact that he sold the shares at exactly the same market price at which he purchased them, thanks to commissions and sales tax Mr. Phelps got back a lot less money than he paid out.

SCOREBOARD

Bought 300 shares of Company A at $4,147.00
Sold 300 shares of Company A at   3,210.00
Capital Loss   ($ 937.00)

Bought 100 shares of Company B at $3,240.00
Sold 100 shares of Company B at   2,465.00
Capital Loss   ($ 775.00)

Bought 100 shares of Company C at $1,806.50
Sold 100 shares of Company C at   1,716.16
Capital Loss   ($ 90.34)

Total Capital Losses	($1,802.34)
Less Dividend Income (Company B)	25.00
Total Losses	$1,777.34

Mr. Phelps had to admit that making money in the stock market was not quite as easy as he had supposed. He withdrew $5,000 from his savings account, invested a good portion of it, made $25 in dividends but lost $1,802.34 in trading. Whew! He would have been better off had he left his money where it was. Now he must decide whether to throw in the towel or try to recoup his losses by reinvesting his money in the market.

Ms. Alexis Scott

Ms. Scott had dabbled in the stock market for more than ten years. For the most part, she had been very conservative, investing mainly in utilities which have been paying very high dividends. Now she has decided to become a little more aggressive in her investing techniques, and at the same time that Mr. Phelps was anticipating a bull market she began to plan and prepare for a bear market. She sold some of her utility stock and decided to do some serious trading. As it turned out, she went after the same securities as Mr. Phelps, though she did not make her investments at exactly the same time or for the same reasons.

Transaction No. 1. Ms. Scott decides to take a short position in Company A. She calls her broker, tells him of her plans. The broker borrows the stock from another account so she can "sell" it at the market price of $13-½. She sells 300 shares.

300 shares at $13.50	= $4,050.00
Fees	100.00
To Be Received	$3,950.00

Transaction No. 2. The company's shares drop to a price of $11.00 and Ms. Scott decides that it is time to purchase the shares sold short; she calls her broker and he executes the order for her at $11.00 per share.

300 shares at $11.00	= $3,300
Fees	83
Total Cost	$3,383

SCOREBOARD

Sold short 300 shares of Company A at	$3,950.00
Bought 300 shares of Company A at	3,383.00
Total Capital Gain	$ 567.00

Ms. Scott made a tidy little profit for herself. On an investment of $3,950 she has made a profit of $567. That is a rate of return of almost 14.4 percent ($567 divided by $3,950). And as only two months elapsed between transactions, that's a 14.4 percent return in two *months*. Mr. Phelps, on the other hand, having played the stock in this same company to go up in price lost $937 on a $4,147 investment. He had a 22.6 percent loss in pretty much the same time that Ms. Scott made her 14.4 percent.

Transaction No. 3. Ms. Scott had a feeling that the publishing industry was in for a time of it and she decided that the shares of Company B, then selling at $17-⅝ per share, were at an ideal level for a bear to make some money in a very short time. She instructed her broker to sell short at the market price.

200 shares at $17.625	= $3,525.00
Fees	89.10
To Be Received	$3,435.90

Transaction No. 4. The publishing company became, as we learned from Mr. Phelps' situation, a takeover candidate and the shares skyrocketed in price. Ms. Scott decided to wait out the news, since she believed the takeover attempt would fail—and it did—but the stock seemed to settle in the $24.00 to $26.00 range and Ms. Scott was advised that she ought to bail out. When the stock was at $25-¼ she decided to purchase those shares she had sold short.

200 shares at $25.25	= $5,050.00
Fees	110.00
Total Cost	$5,160.00

SCOREBOARD

Sold short 300 shares, Company A, at $3,950.00
Bought 300 shares of Company B at $3,383.00
Capital Gain $ 567.00

Sold short 200 shares, Company B, at $3,435.90
Bought 200 shares of Company B at $5,160.00
Capital Loss   ($1,724.10)
Total Capital Losses   ($1,157.10)

As the scoreboard indicates, Ms. Scott, who had gains of $567.00 after her first short position is now in the red, with $1,157.10 in losses.

Transaction No. 5. Ms. Scott sells short Company C at $25-⅛. The transaction is for 100 shares.

100 shares at $25.125	= $2,512.50
Fees	60.39
To Be Received	$2,452.11

Ms. Scott watches the movement of this stock quite carefully. Much to her dismay, the prices of the shares begin to climb in price. But she doesn't panic. And finally the market goes bearish; her stock declines.

Transaction No. 6. Ms. Scott purchases the shares sold short at $20-½.

100 shares at $20.50	= $2,050.00
Fees	51.95
Total Cost	$2,101.95

Another gain! But, for Ms. Scott, two wins and one loss still add up to defeat, as the scoreboard shows:

SCOREBOARD

Sold short 300 shares, Company A, at $3,950.00
Bought 300 shares of Company A at $3,383.00
Capital Gain $ 567.00

Sold short 200 shares, Company B, at $3,435.90
Bought 200 shares of Company B at $5,160.00
Capital Loss   ($1,724.10)

Sold short 100 shares, Company C, at $2,452.11
Bought 100 shares of Company C at $2,101.95
Capital Gain $ 350.16
Total Capital Losses   ($ 806.94)

Once we look at the bottom line, it becomes pretty clear that both Mr. Phelps and Ms. Scott would have been much better off if they had left their money in their savings accounts. But they took their chances and learned at least one lesson: It's not that easy to make money in the stock market.

You

You, too, decide that, what with inflation and the possibility of exceptional rewards, the stock market might be the place for your money. You would like to try a few trades. But you know Mr. Phelps and Ms. Scott rather personally, and they've confided to you that it would certainly have been better if their money were left locked tight in the bank. But you decide to give it a try, anyway. There are a couple of stocks you've had your eye on and you are going to try and play them for all they are worth—or what you think, or have been told, they are worth.

Transaction No. 1. You take a long position in a well-known drug chain, Company A. You buy 100 shares at $26-½.

100 shares at $26.50	= $2,650.00
Fees	59.00
Total Cost	$2,709.00

Transaction No. 2. Two months later you sell your holdings in the company for $30-½.

100 shares at $33.50	= $3,350.00
Fees	63.00
Amount Received	$3,287.00

SCOREBOARD
Bought 300 shares of Company A at $2,709.00
Sold 300 shares of Company A at $3,287.00
Capital Gain $ 578.00

Transaction No. 3. You not only felt that the shares in the drug chain Company A would increase no further in share value, but you decided that the stock would now begin to depreciate, so a couple of weeks later you sell short 300 shares at the market price of $30-½.

100 shares at $30.50	= $3,050.00
Fees	63.00
To Be Received	$2,987.00

Transaction No. 4. As you predicted, the price of the stock declined and you decided to cover your short position by buying the shares at $20.00.

100 shares at $20.00	= $2,000.00
Fees	50.00
Capital Gain	$2,050.00

SCOREBOARD

Bought 100 shares of Company A at	$2,709.00
Sold 100 shares of Company A at	$3,287.00
Gain	$ 578.00

Sold short 100 shares, Company A, at	$2,987.00
Bought 100 shares of Company A at	$2,050.00
Capital Gain	$ 937.00
Total Capital Gain	$1,515.00

As the scoreboard indicates, you have played the shares in the company to go up, and then later you played them to go down. Good thinking! Of course, this strategy doesn't always work; just think of what would happen if after you sold short the shares and the company continued to go up.

Transaction No. 5. You purchase 100 shares of a preferred stock in a major airline, Company B. The stock cost $20.00 per share but was paying a $1.87 dividend.

100 shares at $20.00	= $2,000.00
Fees	48.00
Total Cost	$2,048.00

Transaction No. 6. One year later you sell your holdings in the airline at $21.00 per share.

100 shares at $21.00	= $2,100.00
Fees	52.00
Total Received	$2,048.00

But you also received three dividend payments. If the dividend payout was $1.87 per share on an annual basis, then if you had your stock for four quarterly payments, you would have received $187.00 ($1.87 × 100 shares) in dividends. But, in fact, you didn't hold the stock long enough to receive four dividend payments. You actually only received three-fourths of the annual payout. The amount of dividends you received, then, was $140.25 ($187.00 × .75).

The above is only one method of determining the amount of dividends received. Another method would be to divide the annual dividend by 4 to determine the quarterly payout per share. Once that figure is determined, multiply it by 3 for the case above to determine the total amount received for each share. Then multiply the result by 100 (number of shares).

You did well. A sum of $578.00 from selling long on Company A and then $937.00 from selling the same stock short. You broke even in the third transaction but at least received a total of $140.25 in dividends. Total return on your three transactions was $1,655.25. Congratulations.

SCOREBOARD

Bought 100 shares of Company A at $2,709.00
Sold 100 shares of Company A at $3,287.00
Capital Gain $ 578.00

Sold short 100 shares, Company A, at $2,987.00
Bought 100 shares of Company A at $2,050.00
Capital Gain $ 937.00

Bought 100 shares, Company B, at $2.048.00
Sold 100 shares, Company B at $2.048.00
Total Capital Gain $1,515.00
Plus Dividend Income (Major Airline)   140.25
Total Gains $1,655.25

Review Questions

1. You buy 100 shares of AT&T at $55.00 per share, 200 shares of PSE&G at $18.00 per share. Each stock declines by 10 percent. You decide you need the money elsewhere and sell all your holdings. What is your profit or loss?

2. You buy 200 shares of AM International at $15-⅛. You sell it six months later at $15-¾. Buy commissions are $30.00 and sell commissions $32.50. What is your total profit or loss?

3. You purchase 100 shares of Litton Industries at $75.00, 200 shares of Mobil at $30-⅝ and 300 shares of IT&T at $30-⅞. What is your total cost before commissions?

4. You sell the 100 shares of Litton purchased in question no. 3 above at $86-¼ per share. What is your profit if buy-and-sell commissions total $165.00?

5. You sell 200 shares of Mobil purchased in question no. 3 above at $31-¼ per share. What is your profit or loss if buy-and-sell commissions total $150.00?

6

Making More and Losing More

Investors are constantly on the lookout for ways in which they can make a small amount of money do the work of a large amount of money. If you had $1,000 to invest in a stock that you believed would double in value, wouldn't you like to find a way to make that money triple when the stock doubled?

One way to do this is to set up a "margin" account with your broker. A margin account is one which allows you to borrow the money needed to purchase additional securities from your broker. And it is all done automatically once the account is set up; there is none of the usual hassle the average consumer must go through when he wants to borrow money. There are, of course, restrictions and, depending upon the law at any given time, the amount which you may be allowed to borrow will vary.

You must pay interest on the money you borrow, but this is usually a relatively low rate—*but not always*. The borrowed money in each stock purchase gives you the kind of leverage you need to greatly increase your profit or your income. However, it is also the kind of tool that can work against you—it can greatly increase your losses.

Let's take a brief look at the mathematics. You have $1,000 to invest in a stock and so does your friend, Mr. Phelps. You both believe the stock has a chance of doubling in value in a very short time, so you are both quite bullish.

Mr. Phelps invests his $1,000. One month later the stock doubles and Mr. Phelps sells out. His return on investment before commissions and sales tax is 100 percent, for he has made $1,000.

You, however, decide to buy the stock on margin. This means you can actually purchase $2,000 worth of stock. The stock, of course, doubles and you sell out at the same time as Mr. Phelps, then pay the broker back the money you borrowed. Your return on investment before commissions and interest charges is 300 percent. Your $1,000 has become $3,000. Let's look at how this was accomplished.

1. You had $1,000 to invest in a stock.

2. You borrowed $1,000 from your broker and now had $2,000 to invest.

3. The stock doubled and you sold it. Amount received on the sale was $4,000 ($2,000 × 2).

4. You paid back the $1,000 you borrowed from the broker. You now have in your account $3,000 ($4,000 – $1,000).

5. $3,000 is three times the amount you started with. That is a tripling of your money.

With his $1,000, Mr. Phelps made another $1,000. With your $1,000 you made another $2,000. You tripled your money when Phelps only doubled his. You made $1,000 more than he with the same exact investment!

But if the stock went south instead of north (which is to say that if the price of the stock declined instead of increased), you would have wished that you were as conservative in your investment policies as Mr. Phelps.

For example, this time assume that instead of doubling in price the stock decreased so that on selling out, Mr. Phelps, before commissions, was left with only $500.00. (Stock decreases 50%—50% × $1,000 investment = $500.00).

You however, would be left with nothing if you sold out when the stock had declined 50 percent. Why? Well, look closely:

1. You had $1,000 to invest in a stock.

2. You borrowed $1,000 from your broker and now had $2,000 to invest.

3. This stock declined 50 percent in price and so did your investment. Amount received on sale, then, was $1,000 ($2,000 × 50%).

4. But you owe the broker $1,000. You pay him back and you are left with . . . nothing.

Mr. Phelps still has $500.00. You have nothing. Both of you started out with $1,000. He lost half of his money. You lost all of yours.

You see, margin gives a lot of leverage to an investor. Boy! can it increase profits. But, boy! can it accelerate losses.

Once you have opened that margin account, you only have to advise your broker that you are making a purchase "on margin" and the broker automatically puts up his part of the money. How much he puts up depends upon what the current ruling from the Federal Reserve is. Federal Reserve regulations will change from time to time. Margin requirements are tied-in with other economic controls. At the time of the stock market crash in 1929, investors were only required to put up 10 percent of the money required for purchases. At other times investors were not required to put up anything at all; all money could be borrowed from the broker.

You might wonder what happens if you have purchased stock on margin but do not sell out when the stock decreases by, say 50 percent.

Two things happen. One, you continue to pay interest on the money borrowed from the broker; two, if your equity falls below a given level, the broker will require you to put additional funds in your account.

By "equity" is meant your ownership in the particular stock. For example, if your equity in the stock slides to 30 percent of its value (the other 70% being the broker's money), you will be required to make additional deposits in your account.

Very often what happens is that the call—termed a "margin call"—from the broker for the placement of additional funds into the account catches the investor by surprise and he hasn't the cash on hand to meet his obligation. So he is forced to sell out completely just to cover his position. And to make matters all the more unbearable for him, the day after he sells out, the stock may rise 10 percent, 15 percent, 20 percent or more and he will not be in the position to gain from the upswing.

What also often happens is that the stock depreciates more than 50 percent. In this case, if the investor hasn't the cash to meet his obligation, he must not only sell all of his holdings but must also borrow from a bank, finance company or friends to completely cover himself, if he has no other cash or marketable securities on hand. And he has nothing to show for his efforts but no money and new debt! With a cash account he cannot lose more than 100 percent of his investment. With a margin account, however, he can succeed in losing more than 100 percent. Of course, the potential for exceptional profit is always there, but what is often realized is exceptional loss.

Thus, it can never be stressed enough to the new investor that, while margin is a great means of leverage and can greatly multiply profits, margin can also deplete an investor's equity in no time at all!

Remember the first three transactions presented for Mr. Phelps in the previous chapter? In just a few months he lost $1,802.34. But if he had been buying on margin, he would have been in a lot worse shape.

Let's review his first transaction (see Chap. 5). He purchased 300 shares at $13.50 per share. But suppose he used his margin account to purchase 600 shares at that same price per share. Total cost of the shares (before fees) would have been $8,100 ($13.50 × 600).

Of that $8,100 only $4,050 would represent his equity in the stock.

When Company A declined $2.50 per share, he sold out. If he had the 600 shares he would have lost $1,500 before commissions, taxes, and interest were deducted.

If commissions and interest are included in the calculations, Mr. Phelps would have lost in his very first buy/sell transactions on margin just about what he did in all three cash investments he had made.

And if he had used margin to double his investment capability in all his transactions, instead of losing $1,802.34, he would have come very close to losing every cent he had withdrawn from the bank to "play" the market.

The other side of the coin, of course, is that where profits are made they can be much more extensive if the trades are on margin. In the examples of trades executed for your own simulated account in chapter 5, profits which totaled $1,655.25 could have been double that. Dividends would also have doubled. But in the case of the dividends, the interest paid the broker on money borrowed would reduce or cancel their advantage.

Review Questions

All statements are true or false; indicate which.

1. Margin accounts give an investor something called leverage.

2. Leverage is the ability to win or lose more money with the same investment.

3. Everyone should open a margin account. It is the safest way to invest.

4. If you purchase stock on margin but do not sell out when the stock decreases by, say, 50 percent,
    . . . You continue to pay interest on the money borrowed from the broker.
    . . . You are required to put additional funds in your account when your equity falls below margin requirements.

5. By equity is meant your ownership in a particular stock.

7

Dollar-Cost Averaging

Through payroll or broker plans, some investors take a dollar-cost averaging approach to investing. What they do is put an equal amount of money into the same stock, regardless of its current price, at equal calendar intervals—every week, month, quarter, six months, etc.

This represents a fairly safe approach to investing but it is hardly foolproof. (No investment plan is.) Two major considerations are your willingness to stick to plan and your selection of a good stock.

Where's the advantage in dollar-cost averaging? The advantage is that you buy more shares of stock while the stock is in a low trading range than you do when the stock is in a higher trading range. Meanwhile, as the stock increases in value, you make a profit on those shares you purchased at the lower price.

Suppose, for instance, that you feel, after a great deal of research, that over the long term, stock in the Gyro Corporation is a very worthwhile investment. However, you haven't a lot of money to commit at one time and, if you did, you probably wouldn't take a chance on putting it all in one investment. So you decide to invest about $500.00 per month in the shares.

As you will notice by reviewing Table 7.1, you are not always in a position to realize a profit (before fees). In fact, from August '80 until October '80, if you sold all your shares, you would lose money. In November, however, you were at a break-even point (remember commissions). After December '80, you were in the black (which is to say, you were making a profit).

Market value was determined by multiplying per share cost times the total number of shares purchased. The amount of profit or loss may be determined by finding the difference between total investment and market value.

The market value of the shares of stock are rarely on a

Table 7.1
Dollar-Cost Averaging*

Date	Cost Per Share	No. Bought	Purchase Price	Total Shares	Total Invest.	Total Mkt. Value
5/80	$10	50	$500	50	$ 500	$ 500
6/80	12	41	492	91	992	1,092
7/80	11	45	495	136	1,487	1,496
8/80	10	50	500	186	1,987	1,860
9/80	8	62	496	248	2,483	1,984
10/80	9	55	495	303	2,978	2,727
11/80	10	50	500	353	3,478	3,530
12/80	12	41	492	394	3,970	4,728
1/81	15	33	495	528	4,465	7,920
2/81	16	31	496	559	4,961	8,944
3/81	17	29	493	588	5,454	9,996
4/81	18	27	486	615	5,940	11,070
5/81	19	26	494	641	6,434	12,179
6/81	20	25	500	666	6,934	13,320

one way trip north or south. Prices fluctuate—today up, tomorrow down; the day after, up again, etc. If you play the game of dollar-cost averaging, you need to pick a stock that will be bullish on the long-term—and you've got to stick to your game plan!

Review Questions

Refer to Table 7.1 to answer questions.

1. What is your total profit before commissions if you sold your holdings after the 6/81 purchase?

2. Would you have a profit if you had sold all your holdings after the 8/80 purchase? Before commissions? After commissions?

*Broker- and corporate-sponsored programs offer plans whereby fractional shares may be purchased and the same exact amount of money can therefore be invested each time.

3. Would you have a profit if you sold your holdings after the 10/80 purchase?

4. What is the advantage of dollar-cost averaging?

5. True or false? If you play the game of dollar-cost averaging, you need to pick a stock that will be bullish on the long-term—and you've got to stick to your game plan.

8

Stock Dividends and Stock Splits

In addition to cash dividends, boards of directors may opt to declare a stock dividend or a stock split. Actually, there is little difference between a stock split and a stock dividend.

A stock dividend is the payment of additional stock instead of cash to stockholders. The par value of the stock is not reduced and the percentage of the stockholder's ownership in the company remains unchanged.

In the case of a stock split, the distribution of additional shares to the stockholder results in a depreciation of the par value (and market value) of the stock. The percentage of the stockholder's ownership will remain unchanged, just as with the stock dividend.

Suppose that you own 100 shares of stock in a company when a 50 percent stock dividend is declared. For each two shares of stock you own, you would receive an additional share.

$$100 \text{ shares you own} \times .50 \ (50\%) = 50 \text{ shares}$$

You now have 150 shares and the company has reduced its earnings per share by one-third. If it had been earning $1.00 per share, its earnings record would now be reduced to 66-⅔ cents per share. True, you have more stock; but the earnings per share are lower and that will affect the market price.

In the case of the stock dividend, what happens is simply this: you receive your dividend payment in shares of stock rather than in cash. But you mustn't be fooled into believing you own a greater percentage of the company. You have received a greater number of shares but your percentage of the corporate "pie" has remained unchanged.

Now, suppose that another company in which you have 100 shares (at a market value of $10.00 per share) declares a 2-for-1 stock split.* For each share of stock, you will receive

*Stock splits may be in any ratio: 2-1, 3-2, 5-4, etc.

an additional share, but the par value of the stock (as well as the market value) will be decreased accordingly. The result is that instead of 100 shares at $10.00 each, you now have 200 shares at $5.00.

Theoretically, you receive nothing from a stock split. But what does increase is your potential for profit. In the case of the 2-for-1 split above, each $1.00 increase in share value now means $200.00 to you rather than $100.00. However, the possibility of added losses also increases. Each $1.00 decrease in the price of the shares means $200.00 in losses rather than $100.00. Investors, who usually like to think positive, like the prospect of a split not only for the potential doubling of profits if the stock price goes up, but also because it results in a substantial reduction in the price for the shares in the secondary market, thus making the shares that much more attractive to potential buyers.

Both the stock split and the stock dividend have special advantages if the company maintains or increases its cash dividend per share. In this case, the lucky investor has more shares of the same stock receiving at least the same dividend per share as before the split or dividend. However, it is a rare occasion when the cash dividend per share remains the same after a stock dividend or split. In the case of a 2-for-1 stock split, you will find that the value of the stock will be divided by 2 and the dividend payment will also most likely be divided by 2. In the case of a 10 percent stock dividend, you will probably find that the cash dividend is reduced accordingly.

Investor and company interest in stock splits and dividends differ. The investor, of course, has his eye on the potential capital gains or increased income that can occur. However, in the case of the stock dividend, the company is trying to conserve its cash and also keep the market price of the stock at a more successful trading level. The major purpose of a stock split from the company's perspective is the lower trading range that will result.

It is interesting to note that a company may, in fact, consider a reverse split, whereby it actually seeks to reduce the number of shares outstanding. Instead of a 2-for-1 split, the company may decide on a 1-for-2. With the latter, for each two shares you have, you will now receive one. The value of your share in this case will double. But you would, of course, have half as many shares. You have gained or lost nothing, but the company has at least increased the market value of its stock into what it feels is a more secure trading range.

Review Questions

All of the following are true or false statements; indicate which.

1. A stock dividend is the payment of additional stock instead of cash to stockholders.

2. On a stock dividend, the par value of the stock is reduced and the percentage of the stockholder's ownership in the company remains unchanged.

3. In the case of a stock split, the distribution of additional shares to the stockholders results in a depreciation of the par value of the stock.

4. There is really no immediate monetary value to a stock split.

5. Both the stock split and the stock dividend have special advantage if the company maintains or increases its cash dividend per share.

9

Options and Warrants

Knowing how to keep score doesn't make you a successful ballplayer. Knowing the arithmetic involved in buying and selling securities does not mean that success will follow. There is a great deal to learn about investing in the stock market.

For instance, this book has looked at only one method of getting the leverage necessary to increase profit potential; that was the use of margin. There are many other methods.

Stock options are one. Also known as "puts" and "calls," they can produce large profits or losses from a relatively small investment. A *call* gives an investor the right to buy a stock at a fixed price for a given period of time. A *put* gives an investor the right to sell a stock at a fixed price for a given period of time. Note that such investors are not dealing in the stock of a corporation but in the rights to buy or sell that stock at a certain price and within a certain time.

Let's look briefly at the arithmetic involved in options trading, how individuals deal in puts and calls.

First, a call is issued by an individual who becomes the "writer" of the option. "Writer" in this case is simply a synonym for "seller." The buyer of a call, however, is simply referred to as the buyer.

In order to write a call, one must have on account with his broker the underlying common stock into which the call can be converted, or one must deposit, or have on deposit in this account, cash or marketable securities which meet the current margin requirements. Margin, however, cannot be used in the purchase of a call.

Calls are purchased by those who expect a stock to rise; they are sold by those who expect a stock might decline. If you purchase a call, you have purchased the right to buy the stock from the writer at a specified price and within a fixed period of time. If you decide not to exercise your option to buy the underlying stock within the contract period, the price you paid for the call is lost.

Table 9.1
Sales of Options & Warrants
on Registered Exchanges
1960–79

	Options		Rights & Warrants		Option Exercises	
Year	Mkt. Value	Contracts	Mkt. Value	No. of Units	Value	Shares
1960	NA	NA	75	51	NA	NA
1965	NA	NA	305	82	NA	NA
1970	NA	NA	576	295	NA	NA
1973	NA	NA	984	176	NA	NA
1974	NA	NA	394	104	NA	NA
1975	NA	NA	295	150	NA	NA
1976	7,919	23	256	89	2,872	1
1977	10,899	40	190	112	3,696	1
1978	18,953	60	346	82	5,392	1
1979	22,825	65	755	115	8,301	2

From a table in the *1980 Statistical Abstract of the United States*, p. 545. Original source: U.S. Securities and Exchange Commisison. Values in millions of dollars.

For example, suppose that in the options listings in your news or financial paper there is quoted a call offering for 100 shares of XYZ Corp. at $700.00. The fixed price—called the "striking price"—at which the stock may be bought with the contract is $30.00, and the expiration date is in about six months. You note that the closing price of the stock was $28.00.

Allowing for commissions and the $700.00 for the purchase of the call, you calculate that the stock must reach $38.00 before you can break even by exercising your option. But you firmly believe that the stock has potential beyond that, so you buy the call (and also pay the broker his commission). If in that six-month period the stock continues to hover in the $28.00 to $31.00 range, there is nothing for you to gain by exercising the option. So you let it expire and thereby lose the contract price of $700.00 (plus commissions.)

If, however, the stock advances to $45.00, you can exercise your option to buy at $30.00, then turn around and sell the 100 shares for a total of $4,500.00. Given the contract price of $700.00 and commission costs of, say $150.00 your profit would be $650.00.

Now, whereas the call gives you the right to buy the stock at a fixed price for a specified period of time, the put gives you the right to sell the stock for a fixed price during a specified period. The put legally obligates the seller of the contract to accept delivery of the stock and pay to you the agreed price—providing you exercise your rights within the time limit specified by the contract.

Puts are purchased by those who expect a stock to decline in price. For example, suppose you believe that XYZ stock is in for a time of it and will depreciate rather quickly in price. Therefore, you purchase a six-month put on 100 shares at $30.00. You pay the writer of the put $500.00 for the right to the option. You need not be in ownership of the stock to do this, as you can always purchase the stock at a later date to meet contract obligations.

Allowing for commissions and the $500.00 for the purchase of the put, you calculate that the price of the stock must decline to about $23.00 before you can just about break even. If, however, the stock increases in price during the term of the contract, or does not decline in price enough to make exercising your option worthwhile, and you never do exercise the option, then the price you paid for the put is entirely lost.

But, on the other hand, if the price of XYZ goes as far south as $15.00, then you can purchase the stock at that price, and exercise the put to sell at $30.00. Given the contract price of $500.00 and commission costs of about $150.00, your profit would be $850.00.

One, of course, always has the alternative of trading only the options and not becoming involved at all with the underlying securities. In fact, many speculators do just this, for the option prices will fluctuate widely as contract expiration dates approach and/or the prices of the underlying securities make individual contracts pure gamble or worthwhile risk. A lot of money is made—*and lost*—in options trading.

Warrants are another means by which an investor secures the leverage he needs to make more with his money. Warrants are certificates which give to their owners rights to buy stocks at a certain price within a specified time, although some warrants may be perpetual.

There are many variables which affect the price at which a warrant will sell. Grouping these variables under the one simple heading of "current market value" lets us consider the arithmetic of the subject instead of the economics.

The cost of a warrant is usually very minimal in relation to the market value of the stock it represents For instance, the warrant may be selling for $1.00 and the stock for $10.00. In this case, you can see that a one-point rise in the price of the warrant could only be matched by the stock if it moved 10 points. And warrants *do* rise—and *fall*—faster than their relative common stocks.

Warrants are listed on the stock exchanges and appear in the daily stock quotes. They do not have separate listings as do option contracts. Some warrants are good for the entire life of the corporation; most, however, carry expiration dates. It is important to note that the warrant listings in news or financial papers do not specify expiration dates, should they exist, so this is a particular which must always be checked out before purchase. Once a warrant is held beyond expiration date, the investor is left with worthless paper.

Again, options and warrants are only two additional ways of "playing the market." There are other methods and a whole list of related techniques. But these other means and methods must be reserved for advanced students. So, too, should options and warrants be saved for the advanced speculator; they have been discussed here only to illustrate that there are indeed other ways to tackle the market than just by selling, long or short, securities which you may own.

Review Exercises

The following are true or false statements; indicate which.

1. Stock options are a form of leverage for the investor.

2. Stock options are also known as puts and calls.

3. A call gives an investor the right to sell a stock at a fixed price for a given period of time.

4. A put gives an investor the right to sell a stock at a fixed price for a given period of time.

5. Warrants are another method of achieving more leverage with every dollar that you invest.

6. Options and warrants are absolutely safe investments.

7. Writers of options are usually looking for additional income or insurance against any downside risk from the present market price of the stock.

8. Buyers of options are using their investment as a hedge.

9. Puts are purchased as insurance in case a stock slides.

10. Warrants are listed on the stock exchanges.

10

The Corporate View

To this point you have been introduced to the subject of stocks, options, and warrants from the investor's viewpoint in the secondary market created for these issues through the various exchanges. It might be well to take a look at the market from the other viewpoint—that of the corporation.

Common stocks are, of course, only one means by which a corporation obtains the financing it needs to do business. But you might note that what the corporation is offering the public investor is a right to own a piece of the company and yet have his liability limited only to the amount of their investment.

When the corporation drafts its charter it specifies the number of shares of common stock it can issue without having to redraft or alter its charter. Thus, while a company may authorize one million shares, it will keep a certain percentage unissued to allow it such marketing alternatives as share-splitting, stock dividends, or stock options.

Common stock is very often issued with a par value, although legally and theoretically it is not necessary to affix any par value at all to the stock. The par value is just an arbitrary amount helpful to the corporation for bookkeeping purposes. There is one serious complication that can occur, however, and that is if stock is ever issued at a price less than par value, it leaves stockholders with liabilities to corporate creditors. And since corporations want to keep their issues as attractive as possible to the market in general, the par value placed on stocks is usually very, very low. As an investor, you should pay little attention to par values; the only price you are interested in is the current market price of a stock and its future potential as a source of income or capital gains for you.

To bring their stock to market, corporations will usually turn to individuals or companies which specialize in the marketing of securities to the general public. These individuals or companies are known as investment bankers and they work for a profit which actually is determined by the difference between the price they put up for a security and the price they can, in turn, sell it for.

When a corporation uses the services of an investment banker, as most all of them do, they, in actuality, are asking the investment banker to underwrite the sale of their stock. The corporation is actually selling their stock to the investment banker and not directly to the general public. Once the sale is made, the risk of getting the issues to market lies with the investment banker. If he overprices the securities, there will be little demand and he stands to lose a great deal of money. (But, of course, these investment bankers will protect themselves by sharing the risk with each other; seldom will one investment banker underwrite a security on his own.)

These investment bankers, by the way, have the added advantage of creating a market for a particular stock even after it is already issued. In this case, they take a position in the stock and buy and sell shares at whatever the market will bear.

Corporations will give special rights to those who purchase their common stock, as well as to inhibit other rights. For instance, sometimes a corporation will offer more than one type of common; one may carry voting rights and the other may not. Corporations will classify their common stock in this way so that they can, in fact, regulate in legal manner who maintains controlling interest.

Corporations also issue, besides classified common stock, preferred stock. Preferered stockholders, as mentioned in Chapter 4, have preference over common stockholders in claims on a company's assets. In a case of bankruptcy, after the creditors make their claims, preferred stockholders get their share of the spoils, then come the common stockholders. But the preferred shareholders' claims cannot exceed the par value of the preferred stock owned.

A corporation rarely issues preferred stock which gives voting privileges. However, in some extreme cases, as when a company fails to pay preferred dividends over a lengthy period, the preferred stockholders have a right to vote for a limited number of corporate directors.

Unlike common stock, preferred stocks have "call provisions" which put the corporation in the desirable position of being able to retire preferreds at a stated price rather than to chance buying them back at an inflated secondary-market quote. (The corporation would want to retire stock when its board of directors mounts a campaign to reduce debt).

Corporations may assign certain preferred issues a convertibility feature which gives the investor the right to convert each share owned for common stock. When this conversion takes place, the preferred issues are automatically discontinued.

In any event, the corporation usually finds the issuance of preferreds greatly to their financial advantage. Issuance of preferred stock gives the corporation a considerable amount of financing flexibility. For one thing, the dividends need not be paid when business is down, whereas if the corporation had borrowed money from a bank instead of the general public, in good business or bad the corporation would have to pay the interest due on the loan. (Just about every corporation, however, realizes the necessity of maintaining its dividends on preferreds and will do everything within reason not to postpone payment.)

There are actually many aspects to the corporate preference for preferred issues. This chapter has touched only very lightly on the subject. The important point is that from the corporate viewpoint, preferreds offer a great deal of financial flexibility—which is to hint that from the investor's viewpoint, preferreds can be risky in souring times. It is therefore necessary for every investor to pay attention to the rights and privileges offered along with ownership of any preferred issue.

To be sure, corporations realize that one of the most attractive aspects of stock ownership is the dividend payment. To the speculator who buys and sells frequently for capital gains, of course, dividends have little meaning. But to the majority of the shareholders in corporate America, the dividend means a lot. And corporate boards of directors of blue-chip companies are well aware of this and will do as much as possible to set the dividend rate at a level that will compete with savings institutions as well as to do all that is possible to develop a history of uninterrupted and increasing payments. Sometimes they will even borrow the money to meet dividend commitments— a nice gesture, of course, but a highly questionable business practice simply from a financial (and, therefore, investment) viewpoint. The yield on a corporate stock, however, plays a big part in its trading level on the exchanges.

One might think that a corporation could care less about the secondary market value of their stock, since they are not the ones buying and selling the stock. But the level and consistency as well as the growth of a company's stock all add to the overall corporate image, and in many ways represent the success of management. From a very personal perspective, many officers in a company hold thousands of shares; they want to protect their own investment as well as to meet their responsibility to the thousands of shareholders who depend upon them. So the corporation is quite concerned about the market value of the stock.

In every way it is important for the directors of a company to see that the general public in no way loses confidence in the company or its stock. "The company, *or* its stock!"—that may, at first, seem an unusual statement, but the truth of the matter is that a company and its stock are two different things— but few investors are able to make the distinction. A company may very well be highly successful, yet its stock on the secondary market (the stock exchanges) may not currently be an attractive investment. This can be so for many reasons, the main one being that the trading of the related stock is governed strictly by the law of supply and demand. To give an example, five years ago the projected income for a company might have been so exaggerated that there was a run on the stock and the price per share skyrocketed. Today, five years later, the company may be doing fantastically well but still not performing according to the wild predictions earlier made for it. So investors shy away from the stock, bringing down the price while, in actuality, the company has been steadily increasing its earnings.

Very often the reverse can happen. The company's earnings are down but the price of the stock is going up. At this writing just that is happening in the case of a giant corporation entrenched in the graphic arts industry. *The New York Times* reports that in the current fiscal year the company will lose about 90 million dollars. And yet even after this report, the price of the company's stock continues to increase. Investors have been taking advantage of what they evidently feel will be a turn-around situation; they have faith in the new management team of the company and are buying the stock now because they feel it will be worth much more five years hence. (Faith may not move mountains, but—rightly or wrongly—it moves the stock market one way or another.)

Just as preferred and common stock may move in reverse of the success of a company, so too can the price of the warrants a company issues, a price tied less directly to the corporation's earnings than to the performance of its stock. And just as common and preferred stock issues are a corporation's means of financing its growth, so too is the issue of warrants. When the corporation issues that warrant it is giving its stockholders the option of buying a specific number of shares at a specific price.

Once the warrant is used to purchase the common stock, the warrant is no longer any good. It has been exercised and thereby cancelled. When warrants are exercised, the corporation's common stock is increased, thereby bringing down the value of each share of stock.

While this book is not a text on how to invest and when to invest, it is important for the reader to understand at least a bit about the corporate view as well as the investor's. That should lead him to understand the necessity for investigating the rights and privileges that go with common or preferred listings, the effect of exercised warrants on the value of his stock, and especially the fact that the progress or decline of a corporation may not presently be reflected in the market value of its stock.

11

Summary

The stock market is just that—a market where stocks in major corporations are bought and sold by the public. These markets are more aptly defined as exchanges for, in effect, the results of the thousands of transactions is the *exchange* of millions of shares from one owner to another. These exchanges are not unlike auction markets, in that the value of the shares offered each day—each second, for that matter—is determined by what someone is willing to pay for the shares. Thus, if you own shares which you are offering to sell for $12.00 but the most anyone is offering to pay is $9.00, then the true market value of your stock is $9.00.

Stock exchanges have been around for a long time. They have been with us since the 18th century, when financiers traded not only corporate holdings but many other commodities including slaves. The first exchange in the United States was organized in Philadelphia during Washington's presidency. Today there are many exchanges not only in the United States but around the world. In the United States the two largest exchanges are the New York Stock Exchange and the American Stock Exchange, but there are many regional and local exchanges, also, most of which can be found listed in the financial news under "Other U.S. Exchanges."

In Chapter 2 you learned that stock market quotations are generally in eighths (⅛) of a point. There are some exceptions to this, since on many of the smaller exchanges as, perhaps, the Boston or Pacific, you will find some stocks trading in sixteenths (¹⁄₁₆) of a point, or sometimes in thirty-seconds (¹⁄₃₂) of a point, although such fractional listings as these are rare.

Stock listings in the financial sections of daily or weekly journals tell us a lot about a particular security. We are able to tell from them what the trading range has been for the last year, what the price fluctuations have been during the previous day's trading, what the current dividend payment is, how many shares were sold yesterday or last week, what the current yield is based on the dividend and the closing price of the stock, and what the PE ratio for the stock is.

The PE ratio is the price of the current stock in relation to its current earnings. To put it another way, it is the number of times that you must multiply the past year's earnings to obtain the current stock price, and is therefore determined by dividing market price by earnings per share.

But stock quotations acutally tell us quite a bit more. We can learn from footnotes if there have been special dividend payments, stock or cash dividends, splits, or dividends in foreign currency. We can also find out if the company is liquidating or in receivership, or if the dividend is annual or semiannual. There is, in fact, a great deal of information we can learn from the listings in the financial sections of our daily newspapers.

However, as informative as these tables may be, they do not offer all the information needed to make a wise decision about the purchase or sale of stock. As a matter of guidance, you should note that if you do decide to buy or sell a security simply on the information contained in the daily stock listing, you are engaging in nothing more than outright gambling and the chances are that the results you obtain will be terribly disappointing.

An important item to consider is the brokerage fee which you will usually have to pay to buy or sell securities. This is because unless you are on a special stock plan, you will normally trade securities through a stockbroker who charges a fee for each and every buy-and-sell transaction he executes for you. The exact amount of the fee you must pay will vary depending upon the number of shares bought or sold and whether you are trading odd lots or round lots. Round lots are multiples of 100 shares, while odd lots are quantities less than 100.

Brokerage fees vary considerably. Table 12.1 gives a sample listing of the disparity in commissions between brokers.

To be fair, it must be stated again that brokerage houses differ in the kind and extent of the services they offer, and brokers C and D in table 12.1 are full-service brokers, which is to say that they cater to the investor's need for information

Table 12.1
Brokerage Fees

Broker	100 Shares at $40.00	400 shares at $15.00
A	$35.00	$ 43.00
B	$69.00	$122.00
C	$78.00	$138.00
D	$79.00	$139.00

From a comparative advertisement published in *Barron's*

and advice. The discount brokers, on the other hand, offer little in the way of specialized services.

If you are an experienced investor—and it really takes years and lots of trades to call oneself experienced—your safest bet is with the full-service broker. But if you have been trading rather successfully for some time and understand why you have been successful (and you depend little on broker advice), then perhaps the discount, limited-service broker is the more appropriate for you.

There are many reasons why investors will look to the stock market rather than to safer investment vehicles such as savings banks or treasury certificates. But all of them have the same overall purpose—the investor wants the best rate of return he can get on his money. (For a profile of people who own stocks, see Table 12.2.)

Money from savings accounts or savings certificates is called "interest." Money received from a corporation by its stockholders is called "dividends." Not all corporations pay dividends, however, so why buy their stock? Well, because sometimes an investor is less interested in current income in the form of dividends than he is in the capital gains he may receive if the stock increases markedly in price.

That dividend you and the other stockholders may receive from a corporation is quite often expressed as a per-cent value called the "yield" or "rate of return." When you

Table 12.2
Stockowners' Profiles
1965–75

		1965	*1970*	*1975*
	Totals:	20,120	30,850	25,270
Sex				
Male		9,060	15,689	12,698
Female		9,430	15,161	12,508
Age				
Under 21 yrs.		1,280	2,221	1,818
21–44 yrs.		6,842	10,301	6,814
45–64 yrs.		8,301	13,640	10,774
65 yrs. and over		3,347	4,330	5,800
*Education**				
Up to 3 yrs. High School		3,106	3,566	1,621
4 yrs. of High School		5,344	8,697	6,580
1–3 yrs. of College		4,012	5,867	5,301
4 yrs. of College or more		6,028	9,999	9,886
Minors		1,280	2,221	1,818
Income				
Under $5,000		3,183	2,577	841
$5,000–$9,999		7,592	6,233	2,840
$10,000–$14,999		5,199	9,001	4,906
$15,000–$24,999		2,649	8,272	9,461
$25,000 and over		1,147	4,437	7,158

*For high schools and colleges—persons 21 and over; for minors, shareowners whose stockholdings are registered in accordance with the Gifts to Minors Statutes.

Based on a table in the *1980 Statistical Abstract of the United States*, p. 547; original source: N.Y. Stock Exchange. Totals for each year indicated include additional shareowners not considered in the more detailed breakdowns. All figures are in thousands.

divide the dividend by the current price of the stock, you determine the yield from your investment.

$10 dividend ÷ $100 price-per-share = 10% yield

To be eligible for the next dividend payment that is to be declared, you must purchase ownership of the stock before the ex-dividend date; otherwise, the seller maintains rights to the dividend.

All investors should be aware that there are many kinds of stock that a corporation offers. However, there are two major kinds. One is called "common stock" and the other is called "preferred stock."

As the name would imply, preferred stock gives the owner special privileges which always include preference when corporate profits are distributed in the form of dividends.

The par value that we speak about in reference to preferreds has more meaning than the par value we speak about in reference to common stock. The par value assigned to common stock is of little significance to the market value of the stock, although many old-timers will recall when the par value had some connection with the balance sheet of a corporation. In the case of preferred stock, however, though the par has no direct relationship to the fiscal performance of the company, it is the dollar value upon which the amount of dividends to be paid is determined. A preferred stock is listed as a 5% preferred, or a 6%, or a 7%, and what is meant by this is that the annual dividends will amount to 5%, 6% or 7% of whatever the par value of the stock is.

Investors, as noted in Chapter 5, can "play" the market to go up or down. This is to say that they can adopt the investment perspective that allows them to be bullish or bearish in their strategy. To be bullish means to pay a price for the stock which you expect is lower than its value will be anytime in the future. To be bearish means to first sell a stock you do not own at a price you feel is higher than its value will be anytime in the future—and then to have the opportunity to buy it back at a lower price.

A bear takes what is called a "short" position in a

security. He *does* actually sell the stock before he buys it through special arrangement with his broker. To begin with, he instructs his broker that he wants to sell short on a particular issue:

"Sell short, Mr. Broker, 100 shares of Litton Industries at $75.00 per share."

The broker, in turn, borrows the shares to be sold and keeps them on account until the investor decides to buy them back. When the stock falls to $70.00, the investor may call his broker with a buy:

"I want to cover my short position on Litton Industries, Mr. Broker, by purchasing 100 shares at $70.00."

His profit is $5.00 per share before commissions.

It is all a very profitable game—sometimes, anyway, for you can just as surely lose money by taking a short position as by taking a long position. Neither bulls nor bears are *guaranteed* a profit.

There are additional "games" that can be played in the market. One of these is buying and selling "on margin." A margin account is one which allows you to borrow from your broker the money needed to build your portfolio of stocks. The money is borrowed automatically from your broker once the account is set up. You must, of course, pay interest on the money, but margin at least increases your chance for additional profit. Instead of having $1,000 to invest for a 20 percent capital gain, you might now have $2,000, and 20 percent of $2,000 is an extra $200.00 over what you could have earned with only your own money.

Margin is tricky, can be expensive, and just as you can make a lot more with the additional leverage of borrowed money, you can lose drastically.

One of the safer "games" new investors can play is that of dollar-cost averaging, but it is by no means a guarantee against loss. In this method of stock purchase, an equal amount of money is put into a company's stock at equal time intervals— every month, six months, or whatever.

But note that it was not said: Equal amounts of shares are purchased. Rather, it was said: Equal *dollar* amounts are invested. There's a big difference. The advantage in dollar-cost averaging is that you will be buying more shares at a lower price than at a higher price, regardless of the fluctuations. If you stick to plan, there's a good chance of doing well—but, of course, you cannot pick just any stock. You have to have made the right selection in the first place.

Stockholders may, in addition to being the recipients of cash dividends, be the recipients of stock dividends or stock splits. A stock dividend is the payment of additional stock instead of cash to stockholders; each stockholder receives a greater number of shares but still maintains the same relative number. In the case of the stock split, the "pie" is also cut in additional pieces so that while you do indeed have more pieces, all they add up to is what you had originally. This is to say that if you had 10 shares worth $20.00 each before a 2-for-1 split, after the split you will have 20 shares worth $10.00 each.

There are, however, special advantages to stockholders in the case of stock dividends or stock splits, particularly if the issuing corporation maintains or increases the dividend per share. But in the case of stock splits, particularly, the dividend is often decreased by the same multiple that the market value of the stock is decreased. Nevertheless, as the stock price moves up or down, the investor has so many more shares to bring him capital gains—or losses.

By this time the point has no doubt been driven home that the stock market is an unusual auction place where many financial games are played and where there are many vehicles in which the individual investor can play the game—from stocks to warrants and options.

By options is meant stock options, which are also referred to as puts and calls. The call gives you the right to buy a stock at some fixed price for a given period of time. The put gives you the right to sell a stock at some fixed price for a given period of time. But investors (or traders) can deal in the options themselves and buy and sell them in the same way they buy and sell stocks—as long as they realize the additional risk incurred by the time limit on options.

Most warrants also have a time limit on them. Warrants give their holders the right to buy shares of stock at a fixed price. Prices for warrants are relatively low compared to the market price of the stock for which they are meant and they move in greater percentages (up or down) than the price of the representative stock. They are thus of interest to speculators looking for additional leverage.

Shorts, longs, warrants, options—all of these may very well add to your confusion about the stock market. But, then again, perhaps you have been somewhat enlightened about the sea of financial adventure called "the stock market." If you are confused enough to at least admit to the market's complexity, however, and your need to study it further before plunging in, this book has accomplished a great deal besides teaching you some fundamental arithmetic.

And if you have been enlightened to some degree about what can happen and how it can happen, you are at least better suited for that plunge in case you do decide to take it. In this case, too, this little book has at least accomplished more than your understanding of the arithmetic of it all.

12

Problems for You

Here are some simple problems designed to test your understanding of the material presented in the previous chapters. Use a separate sheet of paper to work out your calculations, or use a calculator, if you wish. What is primarily important is that you understand the procedures required to arrive at the correct answers.

1. Mr. Phelps notes that General Motors Corporation common stock ($60.00) is selling at five times earnings, which is to say that the PE ratio on GM common is 5. He wonders what the actual earnings are per share. Can you tell him?

2. Ms. Scott purchased 100 shares of a 5% preferred stock at $90.00 per share. If the par value of the stock is $100.00 per share, what are the annual dividends she would receive on that stock?

3. You own 100 shares of common stock in General Public Utilities. At its quarterly meeting, the Board of Directors of the company declare a 25-cent dividend on each share of common stock. What is the total amount of dividends you will receive with the next payment?

4. You purchase another 100 shares (and now have 200) of common stock in General Public Utilities on the ex-dividend date. The recently declared dividend was 25 cents per share to all stockholders of record. How much will you receive in dividends on the next payment date?

5. On Jan. 25, Ms. Scott purchased 250 shares of 4% preferred stock at $55-1/8. The par value of the stock is $50.00. At the next quarterly meeting, the board of directors declared a regular dividend of 40 cents on the preferred plus an extra divi-

dend of 27 cents. What was the total amount of dividends that Ms. Scott received?

6. If a common stock is yielding 7% based on its close for the day ($60.00), and it pays dividends on a semiannual basis, how much can you expect to receive on the next dividend payment date if you own 50 shares?

7. Which of the following stocks is giving you the better rate of return, based on its closing price? Stock A with an annual dividend of $1.26, closing at $13-⅛? Stock B with an annual dividend of $2.00, closing at $14-⅞? Stock C with an annual dividend of $.76, closing at $3-¾?

8. Which is the more risky and why? Selling short or selling long?

9. If the dividend on a stock is 76 cents per quarter, how much will you receive in dividends annually if you own 125 shares.

10. You sell 200 shares of stock at 1/16 of a point less than you purchased them. How much have you lost before commissions?

11. In a recent sale of 85 shares of a common stock, after transaction fees were subtracted from buy-and-sell sides of the transaction, you lost ⅞ of a point. How much money did you lose?

12. If you purchase 100 shares of an 8% preferred at $20.00 per share, what is your quarterly dividend if the market price of the stock increases to $30.00? Par is $10.00.

13. You purchase 100 common shares of a corporate stock paying an 80-cent dividend. You purchase the stock at $10.00 per share. Just before the ex-dividend date the stock shoots to $30.00 per share. How much will your quarterly dividend be?

14. What will the sum-total of your quarterly dividends be if

you own 300 shares of XW Corporation, 200 shares of YQ Corporation and 100 shares of ZZ Corporation if the quarterly payments are as follows: XW: $1.50 per share; YQ: $.89; ZZ: $1.22 per share.

15. Give another word for rate of return.

16. Determine the yield for both of the transactions below, each of which represents a common stock purchase.

Cost of Shares	Annual Div.	Yield
$1,800	$50.00	?
$3,600	$65.00	?

17. Determine the rate of return for both of the transactions below, each of which represents a preferred stock purchase of 1,000 shares.

Cost of Shares	Fees	Par Value	Div.	Yield
$ 9,000	$202.00	$10.00	6%	?
$15,000	$258.00	$20.00	6%	?

18. What is the difference between a bear and a bull?

19. Bears always make money. Bulls always lose money. True or false? Is the opposite true or false?

20. Your money is safer in a stock market than a bank.

21. If you purchase a stock selling for $100.00 and it declines in market value by 20%, what percent of an increase in the new price of the shares is necessary before it is at $100.00?

22. Why would an investor be interested in purchasing options? Warrants?

23. Define each of the following:

> *a.* PE Ratio
> *b.* Yield
> *c.* Leverage
> *d.* Put
> *e.* Call

24. There is little risk in the purchase of warrants. True or false?

25. What percentage of the next dividend payment would you be entitled to if you purchase a stock after the ex-dividend date?

Trading activity at New York Stock Exchange, 1981. (Courtesy E. Topple, N.Y. Stock Exchange)

Glossary

Many of the terms listed on the pages which follow have a number of different meanings in business and in law. The definitions offered here explain these terms as they relate to the stock market.

account. The record of transactions for an individual, group of individuals, or a corporation.

account analysis. The process of studying an account to determine its profitability, if any, or simply to determine the extent of its activity.

account balance. Value of an account after transactions are completed.

advance. Borrowed money.

appreciation. Increase in the value of an account.

asset. Any item which has commercial or exchange value. Some examples: money, stock certificates, a car, a house.

at the market. An order to buy stock at its current market price.

bear. Someone who feels that the market, or a stock in particular, will decline in value.

bear market. When the stock market is in a period of decline it is often said to be a bear market.

bearish position. When someone is taking a short position in a security, he is said to be taking a bearish position.

bid. An offer to buy a stock at a certain price.

bid-and-asked price. The bid price is that at which someone is willing to buy a certain stock; the asked price is the price at which someone is willing to sell the stock.

bidding up. Continually raising the bid on a stock as the stock begins to appreciate.

bid price. The highest current offer to buy a given security.

Big Board. The New York Stock Exchange.

blue chip. Common stock in large, dominant corporations (such as General Motors or IBM). Blue-chip companies are usually sound investments because of their earnings records.

board of directors. Individuals elected by stockholders of a corporation to oversee the management of their business. There are "inside" board members who are active in daily operations of a business and there are "outside" board members who are only concerned with policy determination.

bond. An interest-bearing certificate. Corporations can raise large sums of money by issuing stock or by borrowing money. Often the amounts they need are so large that no single investor or institution is willing to lend them the amount they need. So the corporation issues 10,000 or so bonds worth $1,000 each, promising to pay the buyer back in, say, 25 years, while paying interest to the holder during that time. A secondary market in the bonds usually occurs and investors may trade the bonds as they do stocks.

book value. Total assets minus all liabilities divided by the number of shares outstanding.

boom. A time of rapidly rising value.

borrowed stocks. Stock certificates borrowed to provide delivery on short sales.

broker. The go-between who brings buyer and seller together.

bull. Someone who feels that the market, or a stock in particular, will increase in value.

bull market. When the stock market is in a period of increasing prices it is referred to as a bull market.

bullish position. When someone is taking a long position in a security, he is said to be taking a bullish position.

buyer's market. When prices are on a downward trend.

capital. Accumulated possessions; net worth.

capitalism. An economic system allowing private ownership of capital goods.

capital gain or loss. When the selling price of a stock exceeds the price at which it was purchased (commissions included), the result is a capital gain. When the selling price of a stock is less than the price at which it was purchased, the result is a capital loss.

capitalization. Total liabilities of a business including both ownership capital and borrowed capital.

capital stock. See *common stock* and *preferred stock*.

commodity. An economic good. Some examples: gold, silver, cattle.

common stock. Capital stock indicating ownership of corporate assets. Holders of common stock generally have voting rights, although this is not always so. If dividends are declared on common stock, they are only issued after the issuing corporation has met its financial commitments on holders of its bonds, debentures, and preferred stocks.

corner. When an investor purchases a stock on such a large scale that he can actually control the price of that stock, he is said to have "cornered" the market for that particular security.

corporation. An artificial person created by state or federal law which functions as a business enterprise. It may be privately or publicly owned and there are no limits on the number of individuals or other corporations which may own a part of it. In all but exceptional cases, each of these owners are liable only to the extent of his or her individual investment.

credit. Allowing an individual or an institution to use goods before payment for them is made.

currency. Money, though most often only paper money.

debenture. A certificate which serves as evidence of a debt.

debt. Money, goods, or services owed to another.

debtor. Someone who owes money.

deficit. A loss in business operations.

diversify. Investing one's money in a number of different securities or commodities instead of in one single investment vehicle. For example, instead of investing $5,000 in General Motors, the money is divided for investment in General Motors, Ford, Chrysler, some gold, some silver, etc.

dividends. The share of a corporation's net earnings paid to stockholders, although cases do occur when a company pays a dividend out of past earnings even though it is not operating profitably during the present fiscal period. On preferred shares, dividends are fixed. On common shares, however, the dividend will vary according to fiscal success and the amount of cash that may be available for distribution. There are a number of kinds of dividends:

1. *Cumulative.* This is a dividend which if at any time it is not paid in full, the difference is added on to the next payment.

2. *Extraordinary.* This is an additional or special dividend paid to stockholders. It is not paid on a regular basis and is usually distributed as a result of a corporate earnings surplus.

3. *Liquidating.* This type of dividend is usually paid when a corporation is terminating one or more of its operations—or its entire business—and is making final settlements with all debtors and creditors.

4. *Preferred.* This is a dividend paid to owners of special classes of stock called "preferreds." These "preferred" stockholders have a claim on the company's earnings which has a legal priority over any claim by "common" stockholders; they are also usually given priority over common stockholders when a company liquidates.

5. *Scrip.* This is a dividend which is paid neither in cash nor in stock but instead in certificates of indebtedness which give the holder legal rights against the corporation.

6. *Stock.* This is a dividend payment in stock rather than in cash; each stockholder receives a greater number of shares but still maintains the same relative number of shares.

dollar-cost averaging. A system of buying shares of stock at regular intervals with close to the same fixed dollar amount for each purchase. Stocks are purchased by the dollar rather than by the share. In this way, more stock can be purchased when prices are low and fewer shares will be purchased when prices are high. The buyer hopes that the downswing in price that always occurs will only be temporary so that when the stockholder finally sells out, the selling price will be more than the average price he paid.

Dow Jones averages. The average price of certain industrial, utility, and rail stocks which the *Wall Street Journal* uses as a means for measuring the performance of the stock market in general. The stocks which make up the averages appear in the *Wall Street Journal* every Monday.

equities. Another term for common stocks.

equity capital. Money invested in a business by owners of that business.

ex-dividend. This is another term for "without dividend." A buyer of a stock which is ex-dividend has no rights to the coming dividend period.

ex-dividend date. The deadline for determining who is entitled to the coming dividend, the buyer or the seller of the stock. Stock purchased before the ex-dividend date brings with it the right to the coming dividend. Stock purchased after the ex-dividend date is "ex-dividend."

fiscal. Financial activities.

fiscal period. The accounting period of a business or agency.

fiscal year. The accounting year of a firm. Many corporations are not on a calendar year; their accounting year may run from July 1 to June 30, or October 1 to September 30, etc.

futures. Agreements to buy and sell commodities, as well as to receive or deliver them. Futures markets are highly speculative.

gross. The entire income received before taxes or other deductions are subtracted.

gross profit. The result obtained from subtracting the total cost of goods sold from total sales revenues.

guaranteed stock. Stocks which guarantee dividends, though these dividends will be paid by someone other than the company issuing the stock.

heavy market. A market which is in decline because there are many more sellers at each lower price than there are buyers.

hedging. Buying or selling securities or commodities so that one purchase offsets another; it is a way of preventing losses because of price variations.

holders-of-record. Corporate stockholders recorded as such by a firm's transfer agent on a given date. These stockholders are enitled to any cash dividends, stock dividends, or other benefits which are declared.

income. Money due from sales or services.

indenture. A written agreement which sets the terms under which bonds or debentures are issued.

inflation. Rapidly rising prices and a mounting supply of money. A dollar buys less.

insider reports. Reports which must be filed with the Securities and Exchange Commission by stockholders who own more than 10 percent of the corporation listed on the national stock exchanges.

insolvency. Not able to pay money owed.

interest. The cost of borrowing money.

interest rate. The percent of the money borrowed that the interest charge represents.

investment. Using money in the hope of making more money. There is never any guarantee an investment will be profitable.

lapse. Letting an order to buy or sell a security terminate after a given time.

leverage. Letting, so to speak, one dollar do the work of many, as in buying on margin. One example is the investor who borrows $1,000 to purchase $2,000 worth of stock. If the value of the stock doubles and he sells it, he pays back the $1,000 he owes but has $3,000 left. The stock, of course, only doubled but he, in fact, tripled his money.

liability. A debt or service owed.

long position. The position in securities taken by a bull. He buys securities and holds them with the expectation that they will increase in value.

margin. Money on reserve, specifically to protect the broker who has lent money to an account. The money need not be cash but some type of marketable instrument.

margin call. Some investors borrow heavily from their brokers to achieve the greatest possible leverage. The broker has no second thoughts about lending the money because he has the securities purchased as collateral. However, in a declining market, the value of an investor's equity may depreciate to such an extent that the broker may request some payment with the purchase; that request is the margin call. Basically, the margin call is any notice for partial payment of the loan from the broker.

merger. When two or more companies combine.

narrow market. When there is little trading in stocks and not much of a price movement in those stocks which are traded.

National Association of Securities Dealers. Brokers and dealers who handle the "over-the-counter (OTC)" securities.

net profit. Profit realized after the deduction of all expenses.

odd-lot. One to 99 shares of stock.

over-the-counter. Trading in stocks not listed on recognized exchanges.

par value. An arbitrary value given to each share of stock in a corporation. However, no matter what the par value may be—$10.00, $20.00 or $30.00—the real value of a stock is in its market value.

preferred stock. Stock which has preference over common stock in the distribution of earnings. A company may issue many classes of preferred stock, each with its own rights.

profit taking. Selling securities to make a profit.

proxy. A person with authorization to represent another.

rally. An upward performance of a stock, or stocks in general, after a period, no matter how brief, of decline.

revenue. The income from an investment.

risk. When chances of losing money are far greater than chances of making money.

round lot. One hundred shares of stock and multiples thereof.

short position. The position in securities taken by a bear. He has sold a stock he does not own and has not yet bought it to cover his position.

short sale. Selling a stock which you do not own and buying it back—at a lower price, you hope. A transaction like this is possible because what the broker does is borrow stock from another account to enable you to "sell short." Short sellers are bears; they expect the market in general, or a given security specifically, to go down.

specialist. A member of the stock exchange who is, in fact, a broker for brokers and whose legal responsiblity it is to maintain orderly trading in the marketplace.

stock certificate. A printed form which gives evidence of a particular individual's ownership in a corporation.

stock split. Increasing the number of shares to each shareholder. For example, after a stock split, instead of 10 shares at $100.00 market value, you would now have 20 shares at $50.00 market value. The number of shares outstanding increases in a stock split but not the capitalization.

technician. An individual who charts the up-and-down movements of stocks and uses these charts to project future price movements.

ticker. A visual communication device which prints out stock trading results.

transfer agent. An individual, bank, or trust which has been appointed to manage transfers involved in a company's stock.

unload. Selling securities.

utilities. Companies which supply gas, water, telecommunications, and electricity to businesses and individuals.

voting stock. Stock which gives its owners the right to vote for directors of a company and on other matters which the directors may put forth to its investors.

warrant. An option to buy shares of stock at a given price.

windfall. An unusually high profit.

yield. The rate of return from an investment.

Answers to Review Questions

Chapter 1

1. The stock market is that market for corporate stocks created by national and local exchanges around the world. *True*

2. Since the 1700s, small, informal exchanges have existed in the United States. *True*

3. In the early days, stock exchanges not only dealt in corporate stocks but also in the slave trade. *True*

4. The first organized exchange in the United States was established in Philadelphia in the year 1790. *True*

5. The New York Stock Exchange was originally called the New York Curb Exchange. *False*

6. There is now only one exchange in the United States: The New York Stock Exchange. *False*

7. Floor brokers conduct transactions for other members of the same exchange in return for a commission. *True*

8. Registered brokers are members of an exchange who buy and sell securities for their account. *True*

9. Odd-lot dealers are those exchange members who buy from, or sell to, customers of commission brokers dealing in fewer than 100 shares. *True*

10. Block positioners handle trades of $200,000 or more in a particular stock. *True*

Chapter 2

1. The largest exchange in the United States is the New York Stock Exchange. *True*

2. Yield is the annual (unless otherwise specified) rate of return. *True*

3. PE ratio refers to the number of times by which the company's latest 12-month earnings must be multiplied to obtain the current stock price. *True*

4. Convert the following fractions to parts of a dollar:

> *a.* ⅛   (12-½ cents)
> *b.* ¼   (25 cents)
> *c.* ⅜   (37-½ cents)
> *d.* ⅝   (62-½ cents)
> *e.* 1-¼ ($1.25)

5. You buy 200 shares of XYZ Corp. at $20-½. The company pays an annual dividend of $.50 per share. How much in dividends will you receive each year from XYZ? ($100.00)

Chapter 3

1. If you buy 100 shares of stock for $10.00 per share and sell it six months later for $10-¼ per share, what is your profit before commissions? ($25.00)

2. If you buy 100 shares of stock for $10 per share and sell it five months later for $10-½ per share, how much is your profit (or loss) if your buy-and-sell commissions total $65.00? ($15.00 loss)

3. About where would your break-even point be if you purchased 200 shares of stock at $9.00 per share and the buy commissions were $53.00? ($9-⅝ per share)

4. Will savings in brokerage commissions really enhance your profits if you trade frequently? (Most definitely)

5. Must you pay a brokerage commission even if you take a loss on a stock transaction? (Most definitely)

Chapter 4

1. Determine the rate of return for each transaction below, each of which represents a common stock purchase.

Cost of Shares	Annual Dividends	Rate of Return
$950.00	$45.00	.047
$2,500	$125.00	.050
$6,000	$295.00	.049

2. Determine the rate of return for each of the transactions below, each of which represents a preferred stock purchase of 100 shares.

Cost of Shares	Par Value	Div. Rate	Rate/Return
$9,100	$100.00	4½%	.049
$5,000	$ 50.00	5%	.050
$6,200	$ 50.00	6%	.048

Chapter 5

1. You buy 100 shares of AT&T at $55.00 per share, 200 shares of PSE&G at $18.00 per share. Each stock declines by 10 percent. You decide you need the money elsewhere and sell all your holdings? What is your profit or loss? ($910.00 loss)

2. You buy 200 shares of AM International at $15-⅛. You sell those shares six months later at $15-¾. Buy commissions are $30.00 and sell commissions $32.50. What is your total profit or loss? ($62.50 profit)

3. You purchase 100 shares of Litton Industries at $75.00, 200 shares of Mobil Oil at $30-⅝ and 300 shares of IT&T at $30-⅞. What is your total cost before commissions? ($22,887.50)

4. You sell 100 shares of Litton purchased in question no. 3 above at $86-¼ per share. What is your profit if buy and sell commissions total $165.00? ($960.00 profit)

5. You sell 200 shares of Mobil purchased in question no. 3 above at $31-¼ per share. What is your profit or loss if buy-and-sell commissions total $150.00? ($25.00 loss)

Chapter 6

1. Margin accounts give investors something called leverage. *True*

2. Leverage is the ability to win or lose more money with the same investment. *True*

3. Everyone should open a margin account. It is the safest way to invest. *False*

4. If you purchase stock on margin but do not sell out when the stock decreases by, say, 50 percent,
 . . . You continue to pay interest on the money borrowed from the broker. *True*
 . . . You are required to put additional funds in your account when your equity falls below margin requirements. *True*

5. By equity is meant your ownership in a particular stock. *True*

Chapter 7

1. What is your total profit before commissions if you sold your holdings after the 6/81 purchase? ($6,386)

2. Would you have a profit if you sold all your holdings after the 8/80 purchase? Before commissions? After commissions? (Loss before commissions; loss after commissions.)

3. Would you have a profit if you sold your holdings after the 10/80 purchase? (No)

4. What is the advantage of dollar-cost averaging? (Safety)

5. True or false? If you play the game of dollar-cost averaging, you need to pick a stock that will be bullish on the long-term—and you've got to stick to your game plan. *True*

Chapter 8

1. A stock dividend is the payment of additional stock instead of cash to stockholders. *True*

2. On a stock dividend, the par value of the stock is reduced and the percentage of the stockholder's ownership in the company remains unchanged. *False*

3. In the case of a stock split, the distribution of additional shares to the stockholders results in a depreciation of the par value of the stock. *True*

4. There is really no immediate monetary value to a stock split. *True*

5. Both the stock split and the stock dividend have special advantage if the company maintains or increases its cash dividend per share. *True*

Chapter 9

1. Stock options are a form of leverage for the investor. *True*

2. Stock options are also known as puts and calls. *True*

3. A call gives an investor the right to sell a stock at a fixed price for a given period of time. *False*

4. A put gives an investor the right to sell a stock at a fixed price for a given period of time. *True*

5. Warrants are another method of achieving more leverage with every dollar that you invest. *True*

6. Options and warrants are absolutely safe investments. *False*

7. Writers of options are usually looking for additional income or insurance against any downside risk from the present market price of the stock. *True*

8. Buyers of options are using their investment as a hedge. *True*

9. Puts are purchased as insurance in case a stock slides. *True*

10. Warrants are listed on the stock exchanges. *True*

Chapter 12

1. Mr. Phelps notes that General Motors Corporation common stock ($60.00) is selling at five times earnings, which is to say that the PE ratio on common is 5. He wonders what the actual earnings are per share. Can you tell him? ($12.00)

2. Ms. Scott purchased 100 shares of 5% preferred stock at $90.00 per share. If the par value of the stock is $100.00 per share, what are the annual dividends she would receive on that stock? ($500.00)

3. You own 100 shares of common stock in General Public

Utilities. At its quarterly meeting, the Board of Directors of the company declare a 25-cent dividend on each share of common stock. What is the total amount of dividends you will receive with the next payment? ($25.00)

4. You purchase another 100 shares (and now have 200) of common stock in General Public Utilities on the ex-dividend date. The recently declared dividend was 25 cents per share to all stockholders of record. How much will you receive in dividends on the next payment date? ($25.00 You would get $50.00 if you had purchased before ex-dividend.)

5. On Jan. 25, Ms. Scott purchased 250 shares of 4% preferred stock at $55-⅛. The par value of the stock is $50.00. At the next quarterly meeting, the board of directors declared a regular dividend of 40 cents on the preferred plus an extra dividend of 27 cents. What was the total amount of dividends that Ms. Scott received? ($167.50)

6. If a common stock is yielding 7% based on its close for the day ($60.00), and it pays dividends on a semiannual basis, how much can you expect to receive on the next dividend payment date if you own 50 shares? ($105.00)

7. Which of the following stocks is giving you the better rate of return based on its closing price?

Stock	Annual Div.	Closing Price	Rate of Return
A	$1.26	$13-⅛	.096
B	$2.00	$14-⅞	.134
C	$ .76	$ 3-¾	.203 (Stock C)

8. Which is the more risky and why? Selling short or selling long? (Selling short. Stocks can increase, split and increase ad infinitum, whereas they can only depreciate to zero.)

9. If the dividend on a stock is 76 cents per quarter, how much will you receive in dividends annually if you own 125 shares? ($380.00)

10. You sell 200 shares of a stock at ¹⁄₁₆ of a point less than you purchased them. How much have you lost before commissions? ($12.50)

11. In a recent sale of 85 shares of a common stock, after transaction fees were subtracted from buy-and-sell sides of the transaction, you lost ⁷⁄₈ of a point. How much money did you lose? ($74.38)

12. If you purchase 100 shares of an 8% preferred at $20.00 per share, what is your quarterly dividend if the market price of the stock increases to $30.00. Par is $10.00. ($20.00)

13. You purchase 100 common shares of corporate stock paying an 80-cent dividend. You purchase the stock at $10.00 per share. Just before the ex-dividend date the stock shoots to $30.00 per share. How much will your quarterly dividend be? ($20.00)

14. What will the sum-total of your quarterly dividends be if you own 300 shares of XW Corporation, 200 shares of YQ Corporation and 100 shares of ZZ Corporation if the quarterly payments are as follows: XW: $1.50 per share; YQ: $.89; ZZ: $1.22 per share. ($750.00)

15. Give another word for rate of return. (Yield)

16. Determine the yield for both of the transactions below, each of which represents a common stock purchase.

Cost of Shares	Annual Dividend	Yield
$1,800	$50.00	.028
$3,600	$65.00	.018

17. Determine the rate of return for both of the transactions below, each of which represents a preferred stock purchase of 1,000 shares.

Cost of Shares	Par Value	Div.	Yield
$ 9,000	$10.00	6%	.067
$15,000	$20.00	6%	.080

18. What is the difference between a bear and a bull? (A bear expects the market to go down. A bull expects the market to go up.)

19. Bears always make money. Bulls always lose money. *False* Bulls always make money. Bears always lose money. *False*

20. Your money is safer in the stock market than in a bank. *False*

21. If you purchase stock selling for $100.00 per share and it declines in market value by 20%, what percent of an increase in the new price of the stock is necessary before it is at $100.00? (25%)

22. Why would an investor be interested in purchasing options? Warrants? (Leverage)

23. *a. PE ratio* is the ratio between the price of a share of stock and the earnings for that share of stock.
b. Yield is the rate of return from a security, given as a percentage of the amount invested.
c. Leverage is the control of greater amounts of money with lesser amounts. Buying on margin is an example of obtaining leverage.
d. Put is a type of option whereby you purchase the right to sell a stock within a given period and at a stated price.
e. Call is a type of option whereby you purchase the right to buy a stock within a given period and at a stated price.

24. There is little risk in the purchase of warrants. *False*

25. What percentage of the next dividend payment would you be entitled to if you purchase a stock after the ex-dividend date? (0%)